HALLUCINATION

Published in 2022 by Hardie Grant Books an imprint of
Hardie Grant Publishing

Hardie Grant Books (Melbourne)
Ground Floor, Building 1, 658 Church Street
Richmond VIC 3121, Australia

Hardie Grant Books (London)
5th and 6th Floors, 52–54 Southwark Street
London SE1 1UN, United Kingdom

www.hardiegrant.com.au

Hardie Grant acknowledges the Traditional Owners of the Country
on which we work, the Wurundjeri People of the Kulin Nation and the
Gadigal People of the Eora Nation, and recognises their continuing
connection to the land, waters and culture. We pay our respects to their
Elders past and present.

A catalogue record of this book is available from the National
Library of Australia.
Hallucination
ISBN 9781743799543

Publication commissioned by Courtney Nicholls
Publication managed by Hannah Louey
Written by Jamie Grant
Cover designed by Glenn Moffatt
Typesetting by Megan Ellis
Printed in Australia by Griffin Press

HALLUCINATION

TWENTY

FIRST

CENTURY

POEMS

JAMIE GRANT

Hardie Grant

BOOKS

CONTENTS

Part One

IMMORTALS

The Lane

I never really loved my aunt;
in fact, I didn't like her. Nor
  did I like her bullying son,
while as for her three daughters, one
  seemed too much like the other, for
all I could tell. They weren't called Grant

  to start with, though the look each had
was that of my father and his
  family. As a child I felt
ignored by them, and tried to melt
  into the background when we'd visit
the grandmother – lean and clad

  in woollen skirts – who we had in
common. Their talk was all about
  subjects far above the interests
of the very young, obscure lists
  of names and places which no doubt
were meant to form a clear pattern

  of meaning; if only I'd guessed
then – which of course could not have been –
  at the precise weight and import
of those names, I would not have thought
  the teacup-sipping hours on the green
and white verandah such a test

of patience. My aunt, her husband,
and also each grown-up daughter,
   were all architects. Architecture,
the arts, and even literature
   were what prompted bursts of laughter
and allusion in their household,

   where the father, known as Uncle Cullis,
had been close friends since their schooldays
   with a novelist called White.
But I did not possess foresight
   by which to understand what lay
somewhere in the future. A trellis

   with a passionfruit vine was hung
beside the portico designed
   by Professor Wilkinson; fish
swam in the long stone pond, and fresh
   air came in the French windows; blinds
were rolled up and wooden shutters rung

   together. I wanted to be on
the beach, not waiting for the talk
   to end. Those days were forgotten
with the only exception
   being that in outlines as stark
as a sign drawn in neon

4

I caricatured a version
of that aunt in my mind, which I see
   now to be quite unfair. The thought
of becoming her neighbour ought
   never to have occurred to me,
just the same, when my three children

   outgrew the narrow terrace house
where their lives had begun; yet
   the only perfect-seeming place
for sale, located after days
   and months of search, a cottage set
among trees and flowerbeds, rose

   scented and tile-roofed, was one street
away from where my aunt was living.
   The two houses, ours and hers,
were connected by a shady burr
   and berry smothered lane, giving
to both of our yards a discreet

   hidden path beside the railway line;
the lane was a secret route few
   visitors could find. On our first
day in the new house, her lips pursed,
   my aunt appeared at the door, went through,
then left at once. We had no more sign

that she lived nearby in the course
of the next few years. Our little boy,
    aged six by then, would often play
outdoors, and for much of each day
    struck balls with a battered toy
cricket bat, writing down the scores

    in a notebook. One day I came out
to bowl at him, and when I looked
    toward the end of the driveway
my aunt was there in a long grey
    skirt and a scarlet jacket, crooked
over a walking stick – about

    to move away. "Who's that lady?"
He pointed to her. "She watches
    me every day I think she's
nice." Like one who suddenly sees
    a hidden form, discards crutches
and learns to walk again, shaky

    at first, I was able to see
my disliked aunt in a fresh new
    light; it was as though a window
had been set into a wall, so
    as to allow a sunlit view
to appear. Those who can be

kind to one's children redeem
themselves in that way – and yet
  she still declined to come inside.
I was told old Cullis had died,
  then saw her house on the market.
More months passed. It began to seem

  from her absence that she too might
be dead. Walking up the leaf-hung
  lane on the way to work I'd notice
the house remained unsold. Office
  workers, who I would sit among
on the train, made their way both night

  and morning up and down the hill,
but for much of the day the lane
  was deserted, filled with bird-song
and green shadows. It was a long
  aisle of wildflowers and vine
entangled branches, cool and still,

  one afternoon in winter
when I set out for a walk
  to lead the children home from school.
Between two arching tree-trunks a pool
  of sunlight marked the only fork
on the pathway, where a splinter

of brightness dazzled my eyes.
Looking up, half-blinded, I thought
    I could see my aunt standing there:
a scarlet shape beyond the glare
    reminded me of the bright coat
she often wore. Against the greys

    in the fence, the shape seemed frozen
next to her old home. Was it her ghost
    that had materialised, then,
I wondered, beyond human ken?
    It was something one could almost
wish to believe in, a token

    from an unseen world. As I got
closer, though, it became quite clear
    that the form belonged to my aunt
in person, not her revenant
    shade. She had found a knot-hole to peer
through toward the house, and did not

    seem concerned that I'd caught her
spying on it. "I love this house,"
    she said. "I didn't want to sell,
but they made me." No need to tell
    who *they* referred to: her pained brows
allotted the blame to her daughters.

How she had come, on her bad
legs, she would not say, repeating
   instead, as she peered through the fence,
"It's so sad." Birds called from the dense
   bushes beside us, a fleeting
musical tone. "It's just so sad."

9

Demolition

Is this the aftermath of an explosion,
an insurrection, war, or invasion?
Windowless walls which lean and taper
into vacant corners, a yawning crater
with loose stones mounting in a ruined yard
where bulldozers are working hard
to push aside the heaps of rubble.
In other allotments, it seems the trouble
must have caused the owners to flee,
for they are abandoned, long since empty
and overgrown. And yet all it means
is no such thing: the crumbling wall which leans
there has not been recently destroyed,
nor is that gap-toothed hole a mere void:
they are just half-built.
Elsewhere, rivers are choked with silt.
The man in the luminous jerkin
and metal helmet, and those ones working
beside him, are builders, not a rescue team,
and nothing here is as it might seem,
for it is not ruins which surround
this huge expanse of flattened ground
but a series of construction sites.
There have been many days and nights
filled with the music of demolition,
humming saws and hammering percussion.

Tightly packed houses are filling
up the former cottage gardens, spilling
onto the remnants of farmland
and orchards, clinging like a garland
along the new-made streets. Beside
an empty pool a man with legs wide
apart, wearing a blazer and slacks,
talks to his mobile phone. Animal tracks
are printed on new-laid concrete.
Everything in the district is incomplete.
The building continues. Cranes unload
stacks of metal girders onto the road.
Elsewhere, intellectuals come together
to plan society's ruin. The weather
overshadows the shining suburbs, dark clouds
like grey stone buildings; the crowds
who stream into the shopping malls
remain unmoved by malice where it falls,
and the new-made apartments grow faster
than the outcome of any disaster.

Climate Change

Rain rushing over roof tiles,
  lush grass in the lane, loose smiles
on the faces of farmers and gardeners
  in places where former hardness
gains the texture of fruit jelly;
  rain that soaks the roots of every
growing crop and vine, that falls
  in a slow line from the top of walls,

that lets life be restored.
  Yet what lines are overheard
in shopping centres and offices
  except for complaints that the professors
at the Bureau got their forecast wrong
  again, women anxious, for their long
preserved permanent hairstyle
  cannot afford a drenching, while

businessmen in new shoes
  step around puddles, annoyed and bemused.
A drought is broken, and everyone wants
  to complain. Overflowing fonts
at baptisms, and dams breaking
  their banks, flooded towns waking
to a vista of lakes; yet those
  who only days ago made public shows

of sorrow over the starving sheep
  and dust-filled fields are those who weep
now for the people stranded on roof
  tops; only a few remain aloof
from it all, and wait for the day
  to end. Rainbows arch like a spray
of flowers over a radar screen
  where a forecaster works, unseen

by those who rely on and resent
  the inefficient instrument
that cannot always foretell change
  of climate or of weather.
More storm clouds gather
  beyond the ancient mountain range.
The rain falls in a slow translucent veil.
  Vendors offer umbrellas for sale.

Immortal

New Year's Eve. A fireworks display
above the harbour; immense crowds pack
the shoreline. Laughter and drinking
and senseless brawls. Policemen make their way
    past fold-out chairs
and picnic rugs, their flashlights blinking.
The noise is like that of an airborne attack,
    with lights and explosions. Stairs

that lead to vantage points are bordered
by shining faces. Among them, a teenage boy
is caught up in an argument
the police have to settle, and is ordered
    to leave. He goes
off, looking for an unlighted easement
that will lead to where he might rejoin
    his friends. To get there, he follows

a stranger, another boy, down
a laneway and into such darkness
that neither can see where their feet
ought to be placed, in a part of town
    no-one visits
in daylight, the rock-scattered, steep
embankment above a long-disused
    railway siding. Some bits

of what is to follow must remain
fixed in his memory. The ground slips,
and then he is tumbling in air,
bouncing off stones and stumps down to the old train
    tracks, where he sprawls
with bruises and broken bones, aware
mainly of the sharpness of shoulderblades and hips.
    Afterwards, phone calls

and ambulance sirens, confusion
and lights and cameras, a person's broken form
strapped onto a stretcher to be winched
up the cliff face. The next day's television
    news will portray
the scene, as two faceless figures are inched
toward safety's open doors. He comes to less harm
    than someone else may

have done, after such a tumble.
Later, in the ambulance, it seems as if
he is in a dream full of blinding light.
His friends come to find him in the hospital.
    "I was immortal,
I once thought," he will soon write
on Facebook. "Then I fell off a cliff.
    Now I *know* I'm immortal."

Three Cricket Poems

End of the season

The end of the season. Long shadows
deepen the field's green, and grass is gold
where sunlight catches it. With elbows

raised, the batsmen make elaborate shows
of practice strokes, before a ball is bowled.
Two umpires emerge from green shadows.

The fielders are arranged in well-spaced rows,
crouching down as they have all been told.
The sunlight from behind falls on their elbows.

Voices call out clearly, Waits and Nos.
The turf these figures move across is rolled.
The bowler starts his run within the shadows.

A weatherboard pavilion, with its windows
left ajar, has changing rooms which hold
liniments for painful knees and elbows;

beside it sleeps a length of coiled-up hose.
The players on the field will not grow old
until they retire to the shadows
where watchers stand, with bent can-holding elbows.

Ballade of ice-blocks

We bowled them out for eighty-five.
  There was no chance that we could lose.
Our batsmen only should survive
  to get the runs in ones and twos
  beneath a cloudless sky, its blues
over the earth like something rich.
  For the other side there was one last ruse
To rescue them: put ice-blocks on the pitch.

Back in nineteen-seventy-five
  somebody thought they had to use,
to keep their finals hopes alive,
  a strategy that most might choose
  to see as no more than abuse
of sportsmanship, a method which
  all real cricketers would refuse:
at night, they left some ice-blocks on the pitch.

The first of our side to arrive
  brought us the surprising news.
Only one bowler could even contrive
  to find a damp patch the size of a bruise
  upon the turf: the feared speedster Giannikous.
He gave his belt a tightening hitch.
  There's few more terrorising views
than Giannikous with ice-blocks on the pitch.

Umpire, eight wickets fell to Giannikous,
who used that damp patch to bewitch
   our batsmen. We believed we could not lose
until they left the ice-blocks on the pitch.

The catch

It all depended on one ball,
the annual Writers' cricket match,
the outcome hanging in the air
like a simple outfield catch.

Two runs to win, or one to tie.
The last man in, and one ball left.
The batsman wore a blacksmith's beard,
and heaved his bat with a blacksmith's heft.

The bowler bowled. The batsman heaved,
and the ball lobbed softly up to where
a fielder stood – or so we thought, for he
was there, and yet he was not there.

His back was turned. A long-haired girl
outside the fence was passing by.
She wore a striking mini skirt,
and its bright colours caught his eye,

but as they did the cricket ball
ascended in a gentle arc
above his head. "Catch it, Roland!"
voices echoed all around the park.

Roland turned around too late. Like one
aroused while in a dream, he groped
about him, stretched arms out in defensive
pose, clutched, and blinked, and hoped.

Soft-footed as a butterfly, the ball
alighted on the ground. The catch
was missed. The batsmen ran, and ran
again, and so the Writers lost the match.

Is That Your Brother?

My mother's brother, the Spitfire pilot, vanished
over the English Channel at the outset
of the war. An airfield in Kent, close by
green farmland on the edge of a cliff, wet
with dew; the howling engines, and a sky
crowded with menace: he climbed with polished

boots and pressed uniform over the wing,
and waved from his cockpit. The streamlined plane
swept down the runway, and rose in the air.
It did not return. We are uncertain,
still, as to its fate, and as to where,
if it landed, he was killed. Yet the King

invited my mother's family to attend
a function at the Palace in honour
of those servicemen "Missing Presumed Dead".
There remained doubt, at least for my mother,
after the ceremony, where courtiers led
in the princess soon to be Queen. The end

of the century came, and my mother grew
old with her uncertainty, living to tell
stories to her grandchildren which allowed
the suggestion that her brother was still
alive; one child would tease her, among the crowd
at the shopping centre, or in the queue

at the cinema, pointing to each
elderly man and asking her, "Granny,
is that your brother?" But he had not grown
old: the favoured son, handsome, funny,
gifted at games, would never be known
by generations who lay beyond his reach.

His Spitfire banked above the patchwork land
where farmers with pitchforks ran from a barn
to surround a crash-landed plane; it sloped
into clouds like woollen scarves, their yarn
unravelling. If his family hoped
he might survive, such hope was misplaced. A hand

that gestured from behind a perspex pane
was the last anyone on the ground saw
of him; he flew into myth, like many
others lost in that devouring war.
His last day was warm, windless and sunny.
Debris falling from the white clouds like rain.

That Thing

The wind that blew all night had dislodged
a branch from the red gum, or at least
a slab of bark, and it had become wedged
  on top of the garden gate;

or so she thought. But when she approached
the wooden object leaning there
a pair of yellow eyes – two egg yolks poached
  and glazed – opened to stare

toward her. She was disgusted and repelled.
That dead branch was a living tawny
frogmouth: ornithology might have told
  her; but such knowledge she

had no use for, referring to the bird
as "That Thing", as in "Is That
Thing still there?" The words
  formed as though she spat

some foul taste from her mouth.
Plumage of tree bark, recessed reptilian
beak, eyes like golden coins, earth
  brown and grey tones

designed for That Thing to merge
into its background; the bird stayed all day
on the gate, motionless on the perch,
   and then it went away.

Yet her fear and distaste remained
in the space it chose to vacate,
filling her instinctive mind
   with tawny feathered hate.

The New Nature
(Tim Low)

"Chassez le naturel, il revient au gallop" (French proverb)

In the underground carpark
  beneath the shopping plaza
    the swallows have built a nest

at the top of a concrete pillar
  rusty trolley wheels descending the ramp
    echo the cheeping

newborns while the parent birds swoop past
  toward the light
    the human-built structure

is preferred as a nesting place
  to the trees in the national park
    nearby just as possums

lift tiles on people's rooftops
  in search of shelter more secure
    than their natural

habitat rainbow lorikeets flock
  to the kitchen windows and verandah rails
    of susceptible

householders who feed them bread and seeds
  while bandicoots dig holes in lawns
    and native rats

run up the walls of garden sheds
  as if over level ground
    on vacant ground

neglected by developers
  the ancient forest grows back
    as bluegum saplings

while far off the coast where outfall
  pipes discharge the city's sewage
    a colony

of wandering albatross thrive
  on the stinking refuse
    of everybody's lives.

A Walk in the Coal River Valley
with Christopher Koch

Two figures move along a deserted road
at the centre of a landscape of farms
and forest-capped slopes. A single car passes,
its driver raising one finger off the wheel
in the traditional countryman's
salute. The dust on the road is as real
as the images brought into someone's
mind, of the estuary and its arms
wrapped around townships and sheep-grazed grasses,
 waters that have flowed

down from mountainsides, long extinct cones
of ancient volcanoes. Of the two
walkers, one is myself, while the other
is a man who wears a cap one might see
on a Greek fisherman, a man with shrewd
eyes and a subtle grin, the delicacy
of an old watchmaker somehow imbued
in his manner, even if that is not who
he happens to be. Over the fields a plover
 tips its wings and moans

like a distant child. The thorny hedges
beside the road flourish scarlet berries

the size of tear drops; over the hillside
rows of grapevines are covered in plastic
nets, that flutter in the breeze like flags. Sheep
move slowly in a field, touching their thick
lips to the dust-pale earth. A stone house, deep
among shade-giving conifers; beady-eyed
swallows in the eaves, swooping in flurries
    like swarms of midges;

small birds among the vine-rows. Another house
beside the road, red brick with a tower
on one corner – and my companion tells
the history behind the tower's construction,
and talks about crop growth and old wealth.
His knowledge stretches over the fields, a distraction
from his thoughts about the declining health
which means he must suffer from hour to hour.
From far away, a sound of muffled bells;
    a scattering of cows

steeped in long grass; hills named after household
objects, sugarloaf, cap and bonnet, and
beyond those hills the unseen mountains, jagged
as Switzerland; lakes in hidden valleys,
like the waterways of Europe; small towns
laid out and built almost two centuries
before, beside creeks on flatlands and downs.

The earliest occupants of this land
left no buildings or sculptures, and wore rugged
   cloaks against the cold;

and yet while Napoleon was still alive,
while Lord Byron journeyed among the Greeks,
stone walls and bridges, churches and barracks
arose in forest clearings and on the banks
of rivulets – walls that remain standing
to this day. Buckets and watertanks
in cottage gardens; pathways winding
like the quiet voice of the one who speaks
to me now, of politics and income tax,
   the will to survive,

and the hazards of idealism. A hand
gestures as the words take shape in his thought,
about the past and the present. This place
with its contours and its watercourses
has drawn him back whenever he has meant
to leave. A training track for racehorses
behind a modern farm house, shaped like a tent,
prompts a tale. All through his life he has sought
peace: this landscape written over his face,
   Van Diemen's Land.

Make My Breakfast

My cousin's father phoned her,
even though they were estranged,
on Christmas morning, to complain
about her mother.

She would not cook his breakfast,
he said. He had managed businesses,
negotiated at the highest
levels, terrified his staff,

but still he did not know how
to heat a slice of toast.
My cousin drove across the city's suburbs
in morning sun. Leaves on the great trees hung down

like sheets of discarded gift wrap.
At the top of a long driveway
the house was an empty box, brittle
as cardboard. In the kitchen a tap

was dripping as he sat at the table.
"Make my breakfast," he repeated.
In those times it was not unknown
for a man to be unable

to boil a saucepan of water. Instead
my cousin went to the darkened bedroom.
A figure lay under the sheets.
Her mother was dead.

Don't Ask the Experts

The finest medical scientists are unable to find a cure, or even the cause, of many common ailments.

Economists cover pages with graphs and figures, but they cannot explain the behaviour of the economy.

Meteorologists use radar and computers to foretell the coming weather, which is not the same thing as the climate, but their forecasts are incorrect as often as the choices of a gambler.

Climate change has become an academic specialty, yet it is no more than a speculative extension of meteorology.

Judges and lawyers intentionally misunderstand the law, for their own purposes.

Philosophers use their reasoning techniques to seek to persuade us of notions that are not true, one proving that a people who continue to exist are the victims of a genocide, another arguing that it is as appropriate to liberate animals as it is to kill newborn human children.

As a university student in Cambridge, my father was introduced by his tutor, John Maynard Keynes, to the fifteen-year-old ballerina Margot Fonteyn. Keynes knew about ballet, but his repute derived from economics, not from the dance.

Political scientists teach their students that communism is a good idea, long after the fall of communism.

Psychiatry began with a diagnosis that mistook a cellar beneath the multi-storey building that is the human psyche for the house in its entirety.

"The worst lecturer I ever heard," my father once declared, "was John Maynard Keynes."

Restaurant critics praise inedible food.

The films that are recommended most highly always prove unbearable to watch.

My father travelled to Scotland, and booked a golf lesson with one of Edinburgh's most renowned professionals, but all that he was told was "Hit it, mon!"

The wedding celebrant is a divorcee.

The tradesmen who come to your house (after the wedding), the electrician, the carpenter, the man from the phone company, and the computer technician, all are unable to resolve the problems you have called them about, while the roofer and the arborist are both professional confidence tricksters.

The architect designs an extension with a leaking roof.

The chemistry professor knows nothing about physics; the physicist is ignorant of biology; the biologist cannot grasp sociology; the social scientist has no feeling for literature; the English lecturer dislikes poetry; many poets know nothing about poetry.

"The worst lecturer I ever heard," my father declared on another day, "was G.M. Trevelyan."

Planes on Parade

Early morning, the washing line still
in shadow, clothes hanging in a circle

like a coven of druids at prayer –
and while I am standing there

an airliner crosses over me into the sun
and is illuminated, its body like one

of the objects on display
in a museum of ceramics, the way

the light's pottery glaze glances
off the painted curves and enhances

the colours of the airline livery.
Almost at once, the plane is followed by three

more, each moving forward like a spectator
in a queue outside an arena;

the succession of aircraft resembles the parade
of a triumphant army. Inside

all of these passing vessels
the passengers are putting away their chattels,

closing books and zipping up bags,
looking for luggage tags,

before they begin to gaze ahead
like the audience in a cinema, eyes dead

and unable to move. Soon they will land
to return to separate roles, their days planned

in advance. Yet as one looks from the ground
beneath the rushing sound

of these dynamic machines
it is easy to admire the clean lines

and layers of ingenuity
transmuting into safety

the hazards implicit in the law
of gravity. What are they for,

except to transform all of our lives?
As tightly packed as beehives

the metal capsules descend.
We expect, in the end,

nothing should happen; and nothing does
happen. But just suppose

how it would be were someone
to transpose those unknown

innocent passengers
into the messengers

of a deathly passion,
the jet plane its weapon.

Generation Ajar

They cannot open a door
without leaving it ajar.
If they open a jar
the lid is left lying there
beside the cupboard door

that is also left unlatched.
Through the garden gate
they walk, leaving it
to bang in the wind.
All of this is matched

by lights allowed to shine,
fridges gaping,
bathroom taps dripping,
heaters in empty rooms:
the pattern seems to combine

to tempt one into attaching
the title "Generation Ajar"
to those with untucked
shirts and dishes unstacked.
The habit is catching.

Unbuttoned and unlaced,
I hurry out the door.
Is my concern
about this nothing more
than a matter of taste,

or is there a moral failing
in the generation
who articulate
fleeting thoughts
and the deepest feeling

by way of abbreviations
and acronyms?
Among such whims
there is no firm reply.
To confine emotions

to a plastic screen is to miss
the associations
of human connection
that the letters
spelled out would express.

To leave incomplete
a sentence,
a shoelace
or a shirt button
is perhaps to commit

a long-forgotten sin, the one
that Cranmer's prayer
alluded to where
he said, We have left undone
that which we ought to have done.

Part Two

TOO MANY
BIRTHDAY

Detached Retina

"Well, this is interesting," said the optometrist.
On the screen there was an impressionist
version of the planet Mars, its craters, crevices
and canals, so it would seem. "You can see
where the retina has detached itself," he said.
I could see no such thing, only the red
disc magnified by science and its devices.
Yet that disc represented an emergency.

No time to waste. Soon I was in a hospital,
reduced to an object that masked powerful
figures could manipulate at their will.
One told me that the retina resembled
a sheet of wallpaper that was peeling
off. Then darkness, and voices. The mere thing
I had become was jolted around until
every solid liquefied and trembled.

I awoke with a dark band over the vision
in one eye, a band set in motion
by my own movements, not unlike the line
left on a wall by a flood, and over the course
of several days the flood receded to become
instead a ball or bubble, like the one
in a spirit level, bouncing about each time
my head rotated. It was the force

of gravity made visible. Day followed day,
and the bubble gradually dwindled away
until one morning it was no longer there.
One last checkup, in the specialist's chair.
I gazed into a scanning machine
before the doctor showed me a landscape of green
fields against a black sky: the proof of my recovery.
Or was it a new discovery?

Emergency Flight

An uncomfortable bed
that folds like a seat
in business class
on an airliner:
I lie under a sheet

and listen to the airconditioner,
its ceaseless mechanical roar
like the engines
of a jet.
A nurse comes to the door

and I am almost convinced
of being on a flight
to a distant land,
while that is no nurse
but an attendant who might

offer drinks or duty-free goods.
Another passenger is coughing
somewhere unseen
in the dark
cabin. One must think nothing

about the destination.
Instead, imagine boarding an aeroplane,
entering an upholstered
tunnel to settle
into softness while the engines strain

and heighten their pitch outside –
inside, that mounting pitch can be sensed
within each body
before the climax
of flight, all muscles tensed

until roads tilt within the window frame…
Yet this place has no windows,
and the bed moves out
of the room
on wheels, to pass by doors in rows

on the way to a sterile location.
One is tied to a board
as if by an interrogator
for the CIA,
and methodically tortured

with needles, cords and plastic
tubes. Ten minutes seem to pass.
Nurses and technicians
hold conversations
that go over one's head, like class

discussions half-missed by a latecomer.
Then the torturer's board is wheeled back
to where it came
from, and somehow
it emerges that those minutes took two hours. Black

tea is served, along with
a newspaper, but the names
of the figures
mentioned in the news
seem unfamiliar and wrong, like claims

of kinship from strangers. A half hour
goes by, and the paper begins to make sense.
Cables, cuffs and wires
act as restraints
like the guy ropes of tents,

and my body is connected to a monitor
that emits the same warning
signal as a truck
going into reverse.
Night time follows, and morning,

and another night, and this body remains
in captivity, plotting an escape: if that tube
could be unhooked
and the gown
left sprawled on the bed, cool as an ice-cube

47

I would evade the guards in nurse's
uniform and hide in the grounds...
But instead news comes
to the effect
that release is imminent. Sounds

from the monitors are brusquely switched
off. At the desk one checks out like a guest
leaving a hotel. The air outside
feels like freedom,
until the doctor calls for another test.

Coffee Queue in the New World

I sit in a branch of Starbucks
near Brooklyn's Borough Hall
while snowflakes descend outside
softly as airforce drones
to land on the sidewalk's wide
desert-coloured squares. With phones
pressed to ears, nearly all
the faces crowding the café
ignore the garbage trucks
and cabs out on the thruway,
inhale the coffee smell.

It is all very well
giving to charity
I think, handing a buck
to a homeless fellow
who has just tried his luck
all along the coffee queue,
but the civility
that returned to New York
after the towers fell
is a quality to work
with, throughout the city.

With electricity
to power the subways
and gas in the fuel tanks
of those shiny used cars
lined up in frozen ranks,
a culture of movie stars
acting in Broadway plays,
concerts by Rolling Stones,
endless publicity
promoting *Game of Thrones*,
these should be the best days.

But the political maze,
that confuses our world
and breeds new fanatics
just when it might have seemed
a leader who could fix
the disagreements deemed
to lie beneath those old
insoluble party
feuds had turned a statesman's face
away from the petty,
remains as tightly curled.

They come in from the cold
and wait to place orders,
the people of New York,
while I sit at a table
with coffee and a fork.
The world is unstable
and deadly marauders
might appear anywhere
if we ignore the old
social compact. Fear
can breach any border.

For now, that is water
we have long since crossed;
there is nothing to be
done about it. The new
brings possibility
one should look forward to.
The violence of the past
may lead to fresh violence,
but still cannot alter
the gleaming opulence
that has become its cost.

Yet the future is lost
on me. I am unwell,
now, and old. Arteries
spawn thrombosis, and
chronic kidney disease:
the doctors warn the end
that is waiting for all
might wait for me within.
The snowflakes and the mist,
soft-furred as a kitten,
fall like a conjuror's spell.

Too Many Birthday

There was nothing the Chinese specialist could say
when pressed as to the cause of my complaint.
He shook his head and whispered "Too many birthday."

I went out for a walk beside the bay
only to tumble over in a faint.
All that the kind Dutch specialist would say

was that my heart had stopped, the way
a light turns out, before going on to paint
a grim scenario: "Too many birthday."

It seemed that some corruption was in play.
An artery would not work without a stent
was all the Indian specialist could say.

Now, on my breakfast plate, a bright array
of pills in colours like the autumn taint
in trees that change in time for each birthday –

and here it is again, the third of May.
How many more of these will yet be sent?
The only words the specialists will say
Are muttered sadly, "Just too many birthday."

Part Three

MEETING THE PARSON

An Ordinary Fellow

for John O'Sullivan

"Where have you been, John?" One member of our Friday
foursome
had not been around the golf club for a fortnight.
No-one usually noticed him,
apart from sensing the awesome
power of his tee-shots, and the way
they curved to the right
to end up blocked out by some overhanging limb.

John himself was a mild and unassuming chap,
polite
and spectacle-wearing, with an average frame,
who, like us all, had good days
and bad, and who others might
not even know without his cap.
Even his surname
was unremarkable. Still, he was always

there. Where else would he go? Except for the golf, what
meaning
did daytime hold for us golfers? "Where have you been?"
"I've been to Copenhagen," he
replied, looking up from cleaning
a Titleist in the ball-washer that
stood beside the green.
"What on earth for?" "An awards ceremony

for inventors." We all laughed at that. Why would
one go
to such an event? "I was named on the shortlist
for a prize." "And did you win?"
"Well, actually, I did." So
he had to have invented
something; to persist
in our questioning we began to imagine

what kind of invention such an ordinary
fellow
might have come up with, some painless mousetraps
or accessories for hi-fi
players, an anti-snore pillow
or innovative machinery
for the farm, perhaps…
But then he silenced us. "I invented Wi-Fi."

Nabokov

Berries, beetles and bees
float on the surface of the pool.
I scoop them out with a net
but then more of them fall

onto the still surface.
Birds swoop out of the tree
and dip their wings in the glaze
then shrug and fly away

like somebody dipping in
to the conversational lake
at a tiresome formal function,
a wedding or a wake,

and a black-winged butterfly
like a girl in a cocktail dress
hovers among the leaves
hesitating unless

a predator swallows it whole;
a hydrangea bush nearby
becomes a woman's floral gown
from the corner of my eye.

With the pool scoop in hand
I feel for an instant
like Nabokov holding
a butterfly net, intent

on the capture of a specimen
to pin down on the page,
before that half-glimpsed woman
resolves as an image.

Lyrebird at Christmas

Christmas Day in Melbourne, in the year
of the Great War's centenary – the War
to end all Wars, that failed to end
any conflict. Bored with her extended
family, my younger daughter commands
"Take me somewhere scenic." The sands
of sweeping beaches are too far
for late afternoon in a car.

Instead, I choose to drive her to the forest,
remembered from childhood visits
and school excursions, that I imagined
once as a tropical jungle, drenched
in monsoon rains and hidden fern
trees. Growing older, I was to learn
that the tropics are elsewhere, like the woods
of Europe's fairytale childhoods.

The mountain forest, we schoolboys were told,
concealed tunnels and disused gold
shafts, dangerous for children to enter.
It could also be home to an unseen singer,
the almost mythical lyrebird, or so
the teachers said. Over many visits, no
sign of that bird's presence was apparent,
not even to a long-patient parent.

The highway to the mountains passes
the new suburbs, the malls and business
parks, at last arriving at a boom gate
under the trees where we hesitate
before turning into the picnic grounds.
The tables swarm with unanticipated crowds.
To stay at home with the family on Christmas Day
was always, once, the Australian way.

That way no more, it seems. A whole series
of picnics is in progress, held in ethnic categories:
a group of Arabs, the young men playing
soccer on a hillside, and women wearing
the garment with the resemblance to Nolan's
Ned Kelly, while elsewhere there are Asians
cooking something that smells aromatic,
their children sharing an Aussie Rules kick-to-kick.

Signposts and information boards edge
us toward the forest, over a footbridge
and into the stands of mountain ash
with undergrowth of bracken, ferns, and a fresh
scent of eucalyptus oil. A tourist
descends past us on the sloping forest
pathway. There are birdcalls and running water,
a kookaburra's laughter.

We climb further uphill, and deeper
into the forest. A fallen trunk like a railway sleeper
straddles the creek, before a fork
in the pathway, where the best way to walk
must be chosen – but there on the path
before us stands a lyrebird, no myth
but a living bird, pecking around
at the leaf litter on the ground.

A bird the size of a domestic hen,
its colour an undistinguished brown,
trailing behind it a bundle of plumes
like the train of a bride. But for whom
is the bridal image meant? A future
divorcee? Right in front of us the rare creature
looks up and walks across the path.
A tourist takes a photograph.

A Very Hale Old Gentleman

Montacute village, in Somerset, is built
of Ham Hill stone, and seems to comprise
little more than a grocer's shop, an inn,
a church, and the vicarage across the lane
from the grand mansion Montacute House.
The river Yeo, nearby, is clogged with silt

as it meanders over an open plain
toward the town of Yeovil. In the late
nineteenth century the vicarage
was home to five Powys brothers, in an age
when the vicar's sons would fill in the daylight
hours at play with the family of the Squire. Hay wains

and sycamore trees in the private park
surrounding the great house diverted the boys
who would grow into novelists. Llewelyn,
the youngest, evoked the honey-coloured stone
in a book called *Somerset Essays*;
one of the brothers left no mark

because he died too young, his memories
of their childhood intact. The vicar
and his sons were at times overshadowed
by village tales about an earlier good,
kind man, the previous incumbent, from as far
back in time as that long century's

commencement, who was the Reverend
William Langdon, father of that ancestor
of mine who settled in Van Diemen's Land.
This clergyman was said to have been present
at an election evening dinner
where he joined in a drinking song to end

the proceedings – the famous old song
"Nottingham Ale". "We get the impression,"
wrote Powys, "of a very hale old
gentleman," quoting what the reverend told
a Royal Commission into the conditions
at Ilchester Gaol. There was nothing wrong,

in his opinion, with a clergyman
singing that tune: "I should not be ashamed
to sing it before a Bench of Bishops."
On the other hand, he thought that perhaps
music played by the gaoler (who was named)
to the inmates, along with banners and bandsmen,

was another matter: "I can't say
I should think it was right." One can hear
the voice of my distant forebear, passed
down through two centuries until at last
it has its sound recorded, as it were,
in these pages we still can read today.

"How old are you?" he was asked, and he replied
"In my eighty-second year." In response
to another question he stated proudly
"My son is a lieutenant in the Navy."
The printed answers breathe a sense
of his time. Four years later, he died.

Pheasant for Lunch

"You'll get over him if you spend a year
abroad," my mother was told by her parents.
The possible husband she fancied, it was clear,
was quite unsuitable: a garage

worker whose family were in trade.
If she wanted to marry, at her age,
no impulsive decisions should be made.
England was "Home". It was just a "stage"

she was going through, and beside all that
the young man did not belong to a branch
of the Armed Forces, making him an unfit
match for the daughter of an admiral. Lunch

on the verandah, and tea in the drawing
room: it was all decided. My mother
sailed next week. The sea air, restoring
rest in a deck chair, and nothing other

than games of shuttlecock and reading
to pass the time. The passenger ship
arrived at port, where all roads were leading
to a world of harmless diversions, the shops

and theatres of London. It was a world
at peace, her parents assumed. But instead
the war began before she could unfold
the clothing from her suitcase on the bed.

It was not possible to return
to the safety of Australia.
Meantime, her parents were in Britain
as well, while the unsuitable garage worker

arrived as a member of the Air Force.
He also had a degree from Cambridge,
so now her parents thought that of course
he was suited after all. The marriage

was arranged without delay, a booking
made with the vicar of an old stone church,
the white gown sewn and embroidered, the wedding
cake baked – but then the Blitz came with a lurch;

the hallowed stones were scattered by a bomb,
and the vicar was killed. The church hall
still stood next door, and the curate had come
to survive, so that a hasty phone call

was made to ask the curate to perform
the wedding ceremony, in the dust
and broken glass of the hall. The groom
had to travel by train from Shetland, dressed

in a new-minted Air Force uniform.
London lay in ruins, its factories
and houses, offices and churches, torn
apart and smoking, the ancient trees

in gardens uprooted as if by a storm.
The groom changed trains in Edinburgh. It was a pleasant
day to be waiting on a railway platform.
"For lunch," he later recalled, "I ate a pheasant."

Meeting the Parson

When my father died
the first thing my mother said

was, "Good. Now I can
have a new kitchen."

My sister said, "At last
the old tyrant

is gone." On the day
of his funeral I

and my brothers
came together

to meet with the Anglican
clergyman

who was to lead
the service – he'd

not known the deceased
and the least

we could do
would be to

help him prepare
the homily. Where

to begin? As the oldest,
I spoke first.

"Our father was always fair-minded,"
I said. "He tried

to make each one of us
feel as though we were his

favourite."
"That's not right,"

interrupted the youngest brother.
"I was never

the favoured one. In fact
I was the opposite.

Whatever I did
he disapproved."

"Well," I went on,
"he was gentle.

71

No matter how
we misbehaved he'd show

no violence to us – he
never raised a hand to me…"

The middle brother spoke up before
I finished. "You're

wrong about that.
When I mishit

a ball into his seedlings
he gave me a beating

I've never forgotten."
"All right, I am mistaken.

Yet his speech was gentle.
'That's not very sensible'

was his harshest
admonishment…"

"Gentle?" said the middle brother.
"Not our father.

He was the most abrasive
character I have

ever encountered.
He uttered

whatever he was thinking
without regard for feelings

or sensitivities.
Of course his

tone could be jocular,
but he never left it unclear

when he meant
to offend."

"I am starting,"
said the parson,

"to feel
somewhat grateful

that I never met
the man. Yet

I have to think
of something

to say."
"There must be a way."

And as for me,
I began to see

my clear recollection
as an illusion;

I was like the parson,
disturbed by someone

unknown, sitting
alone in the bare kitchen.

Legion d'Honneur

The first woman among the Allied forces
who came to liberate Paris at the end
of the Second World War happened to be
my mother – although at that time, of course,
she was yet to become a mother. She
belonged, instead, to the WAAF, tasked to send

messages in code as a signals
officer. The city seemed untouched by
the war, the wide nineteenth century
boulevards, the monuments and cathedrals,
buildings that survived their own history,
the Eiffel Tower intact as a New York sky

scraper – all had been spared, it was rumoured,
by the order of Hitler himself. The Germans
had left by the time my mother arrived,
and the Parisians were good-humoured,
on the whole, as most of them had lived
through the invasion in the way that humans

do, acting as though nothing much had changed.
But then the Germans came back, and that,
said my mother, was "quite interesting".
There was a day when she had arranged
a rendezvous with her commanding
officer in an area patrolled by flat

eyed teenage boys, who were Resistance
fighters, hunting for collaborators
to punish in their way: they liked to rape
the women, and cut off their hair. From a distance,
to those boys, it appeared the horseshoe-shape
shoulder-flash that she wore had the letters

AUTRICHE, or Austria, rather than
AUSTRALIA. She was seized, and about
to be stripped and shaved, for the young boys
in their ignorance did not know the German
for Austria begins with an O; the noise
of the incident fortunately brought

some Allied troops to the rescue.
                         After
that, life went on, and seventy years went past.
To celebrate the centenary of Anzac
Day, the French Government made a gesture
toward the Australians who came back,
and who were still alive, with the highest

of their honours, the Legion d'Honneur.
Among the Chevaliers, my mother
was the only woman. A ceremony
took place in an underground lecture
theatre beneath the Shrine of Remembrance. As many
wheelchairs and walking frames and other

aids to mobility as the motors
in peak hour traffic cluttered the foyer
outside the sloping auditorium
where the French Ambassador pinned honours
on two dozen nonagenarian
former soldiers as well as my mother

in her best dress, mispronouncing most
of their names, and describing warfare
as "Ell". Young men who had marched in formation
along tree-lined roadways while the French dust
coated their boots, or proved a nation's
mettle as fearless pilots in the air,

were reduced now to quavering, mottled
near-skeletons unable to stand for
the anthem. Yet when they noticed
a female in their company they battled
one another for her attention, enticed
to rekindle lechery even war

could not extinguish. Each one in turn
spoke softly to her, leaning on stout canes
or metal frames, and she was delighted
by the evidence that she could still earn
such tough-whiskered masculine lust, however belated.
Outside, the skyline was bristling with cranes.

Allergies

As a very small boy, before my memory
begins, I was prone to skin complaints
and other reactions. Given the allergy
test, where a doctor paints

the essence of various substances
over a series of scratches down one's back,
I turned out to be sensitive
to almost everything, from haystacks

and pollens to house-dust, mould,
eggs, milk, and animal products such as cat,
dog and horse hair. The specialist told
my parents that

they would need to rid their home
of all these things. My father smiled.
"Wouldn't it be easier," he asked, like an evil gnome,
"to get rid of the child?"

The Written Word

The spoken word can sometimes be forgotten,
but phrases carefully set out in hard
clear script, once written, can never be unwritten.

Thus, at the end of a marriage, and at the end
of more than two decades, a wife presented
her soon-to-be former husband

with a children's exercise book, in which
all of his offences against her had
been recorded, set out in each

case in careful handwriting, where an instance
would be underlined, sometimes, and linked
by arrows or stars to a previous offence,

such as: *November 20. Late to come
home, without notice* which was connected
to: *Once again did not come home,*

the two examples being more than ten years
apart. The infractions he remembered
clearly: office functions, with beers

and the last train missed, and he knew as well
that his guilt was never to be questioned,
nor would it have helped to tell

her that most of the crimes were trivial:
Dishwasher – again – incorrectly stacked.
Accumulating over several

years, they had assumed the weight of scripture.
The pages were clean, uncluttered and lined.
There was a kind of rapture

Of hatred in every black ruled line.
Yet all that he had wanted, he explained,
was to give her happiness. No crime

however diligently recorded
ought to outweigh, he considered,
the sincerely intended

kindness behind every inadvertent sin.
For her, however, his intentions carried
no weight. Everything was in

the book. The written word amounted to proof
and could not be contradicted.
A black and white bird on the roof

its plumage the colour of print
cried out in a voice like a child
its eyes hard as polished flint.

My Carrot

Always in pairs
the rainbow

lorikeets
tap on the glass

to demand
prompt service

masterful
as a wealthy patron

in an exclusive
restaurant

summoning
the waiter

with a nod.
The colours

in their plumage
are those of

the spectrum,
scarlet, yellow

and blue
against a leaf-green

background,
suggesting

opulence
and power

and they are
powerful,

feared by all
other birds

for their sharp
scimitar-curved

beaks
and for the way

they move
in tight groups

like Roman
phalanxes.

They mingle only
with their own

kind
and hence

they practise
racism,

breeding purity
like Nazis.

At sunset
they gather

in the branches
of a conifer

screaming like
a playground

of primary school
students,

their bright colours
invisible

amid the darkening
foliage;

in daylight
they hurtle

like missiles
at head height

or hover over
pollen-weighted

camellia blooms
soft-footed

as butterflies,
unafraid

of any human
presence.

Muttering
to one another

in tones that sound
like the creak

of an unoiled
garden gate

they shimmer
with the pure

significance
of the entirely

insignificant.
A lorikeet

is perched
on a limb

within a child's
arm-length:

the two-year-old,
possessive

by nature
despite a still

incomplete
vocabulary,

insists "This one's
my carrot."

Lone Wolves

Autumn's rust
in the trees
and drizzle
on the screen

the city's outskirts
housing estates
with cul-de-sacs
fitted like jigsaw

puzzle pieces
the countryside
under growing cloud
rock cuttings

and gorges
fences and hills
plains level
as the sea

wood fires
in farm kitchens
lakes and tree
lined dams

grazing cattle
with varied patterns
on their backs
something black

fills the rear
view mirror
insects perhaps
crawling on glass

like the swarm
of bees that forms
on a bough
in the garden

swelling and humming
with threat
the blackness spreads
a liquid spill

or something
organic
a tumour
on an X ray

filling the mirror
until the view
overflows
with a mass

like a crowd
murmuring
outside a stadium
motorcyclists

in black leather
uniforms
tattooed and bearded
a lawless

regiment
on the march
rushing toward
the car

as a wave
rolls up the beach
to break
around one's ankles

the engine roar
like thunder
of breaking surf
the cyclists

pass on both sides
at high speed
each one's leathers
emblazoned

with the title Lone Wolf
they recede
beyond a hill
as rising sun burns

the last autumnal mist
from the plains
and grazing
high clouds.

Epitaph

for Tim O'Brien (1995-2016)

Seabirds at sundown skim
toward the horizon's glassy rim;
the day's pure light grows dim
as we remember him.

The echo of his name
like a wind-blown flame
gutters in the frame
of the gateway we all came

through to find this place.
The teeming human race
now occupies less space
in the absence of his face.

The birds remain unmoved
that someone who was loved
should have been removed
from ground they swoop above,

and their indifference
converts his absence
into a cheering sense
of eternity's present tense.

Wind Farm

Propellers of an oversized aircraft
planted above the shoreline

the blades turn over
slowly as the hands of a clock

mounted on windowless towers
tall as lighthouses

and glossy as a jetliner.
Seen from a distance

the towers bristle
like the spines of an anteater

or like the white dead
tree trunks

left over the hillsides
by a bushfire;

closer up
they reveal

artistic curves
and marble-smooth textures,

pure as sculpture;
they could be the icons

of a long-lost
religion, or goal-posts

of an obscure
sport, no longer played.

Visitors from the future
may wonder at them,

as we wonder
at those giant

Easter Island statues,
not seeing their purpose

as the latest expression
of humanity's

centuries-old dream:
a workable

perpetual motion machine.

In Flames

Slack water beneath the creaking pier
where children lean on a wooden rail
and scatter chips and breadcrumbs.
We are about to sail,

but first we watch the fish jostle
one another, like shoppers at the mall,
to gather the fallen crumbs.
Then it is time for us all

to climb aboard the yacht,
with its furled sails and motor idling.
The journey begins, downstream,
the boat sidling

beneath forest-shadowed banks
and sandstone cliffs, the blue-green hills
looming like clouds above the mast.
The world of work and bills

is left behind as we relax
on deck, the glamorous boat-owners
and us, sipping champagne
and, as a bonus,

the children distracted and content
to play with one another
allowing us to converse
with their young mother,

who is pleased with her beauty
like many doctors' wives,
and her husband, the trusted GP,
who holds human lives

in his grasp and is aware of it. He
basks in the light draped over the stern
as he basks in the admiration,
glowing like sunburn,

of his patients with their imaginary
ailments. Flaunting borrowed wealth
dependent on those people
and their constant ill-health,

he is playing the part, today,
of family man and host,
and the yacht slides onward
like a ghost.

We open a picnic basket
on the deck, and hand out cans of Coke
to the children. As we eat
someone smells smoke.

Ash-white clouds are rising off the hills.
The sun is now a burnished metal plate.
Unless we return to the shore
it may be too late.

The boat turns and is headed
upstream once more. Soon there are flames
among the forested banks.
The children's games

are over. A tunnel of fire
seems to surround us. Our doctor friend's
calm bedside manner
abruptly ends,

while his elegant wife
cannot disguise her disdain,
for it is not the forest but their marriage
going up in flames.

Drowned Sailors

At my mother's ninetieth birthday party
a cousin of hers I had never met before
spoke about my uncle (he was present,
out of earshot). I had known him as a hearty
and urbane godfather, a visitor
who never stayed for long, always being sent

on exotic naval postings around
the world. "When he was young he was so
beautiful," the cousin said. "I had such an urge
to stroke him – but doing that, I found,
made my mother angry: 'You know
you must not touch *men,'* she said." Some large

plates appeared on the buffet. "He got married
during the War, but that soon ended in
divorce when he was noticed leaving a hotel
with a lady not his wife." The divorce had
no adverse effect on his prospects then,
as a succession of promotions tell

of a steady rise: lieutenant, commander, captain.
"He was a charmer, " said the cousin. I looked
across the room. There, the handsome figure
she described sat reduced to a ruin,
half-blind, unable to walk, crooked
over the table like an ancient beggar,

but someone was laughing at a remark
he had made. Speeches would follow, and dinner
was approaching. His second wife perched beside him
as if a miniature, speechless and dark
with the bitterness of senility, thinner
than ever, like a big-eyed famine victim,

no longer the glamorous TV actress
she had once claimed to be, speaking in
a faint American accent with her
new relations who would think less
of her after finding she was no American.
All the same, she would snarl like a tiger

in defence of her husband when he was blamed
wrongly for the sinking of an allied
destroyer, and she raised her children
with a tigerish intensity, aimed
at discipline and character. Seated beside
his uncle at the party the youngest son

in our family, master of ceremony and speech
maker, heir to that uncle's charm if not
his beauty, condensed the long life story
of our mother into platitude, until each
guest yawned and fidgeted. I adjusted the knot
of my tie. A different memory

came to me, of a weekend I had been
sent to stay with my uncle at the land-based
naval school where he was commander.
The base was all red-brick buildings and green
lawns, beside Westernport Bay. The taste
of salt was in everything, even the air;

and I was left on my own by my host,
who was much too busy to entertain
a godchild. I sensed indifference
beneath the easy charm that was his most
admired quality. I thought about the train
that would take me away, and the wire fence

around the perimeter; I only thought
of myself, ignorant of the coming
night that would transform many futures,
two great vessels crossing, starboard to port,
in the darkened sea, and metallic screaming,
and waves scattered with drowned sailors.

Morte d'Arthur

"I forbid you to buy
that dog." The instruction
could not be mistaken.
And yet it was taken
in the opposite direction.
Later the same day
a return to the pet shop
brought a yellow-furred,
soft-nosed, eyesight-blurred
retriever pup

into the home. A name
was chosen, that might be deemed
suited for a middle-rank
suburban bank
employee, for it seemed
we live in a time
where people give to their pets
the names they once gave
their children, and save
more animal epithets

for children who then grow
up to be teased at school
for a label
they had been unable
to choose, uncool
or comical. It happened, also,
that the name given
to the puppy was that
of a mythical king. At
the end of seven

dog years, a year had passed
for his human owners,
and in that stretch
of time he learned to fetch
a ball and chew on bones
for dinner and at breakfast.
Once he was captured
by council rangers
approaching strangers
on a railway platform.

He pursued possums
in the trees, and barked
at passers-by
from behind the safety
of a fence, chased parked

cars, rolled in algae blossoms
from the pool, and lay
across the doorstep
as if meaning to stop
intruders, until the day

when he moved himself inside,
becoming as much a part
of the furniture
as the rugs and feature
window. He was smart
enough, by then, to hide
his half-chewed bones
in shaded spots
where he would not
forget the ones

putrid with clinging
soil-coated meat.
He lay before
the winter fire
in dream-twitched sleep,
his hair moulting
on carpet
and floorboard
alike. The word
"dinner" would set

him prancing
from paw to paw
with visible pleasure,
a measure
of animal greed, before
he went hunting
for scent among the trees.
He had a perfect life
for a dog, but like all life
it could not be

eternal. At the end
he became confused
like Henry James in his
final illness
who was convinced
that his London apartment
was really a ship at sea
while his kind support
staff were all part
of a conspiracy;

in his canine
bewilderment
our old dog kept mistaking
walls for doors, and walking
in circles when he meant

to take a straight line.
There was nothing to be done,
said the vet,
but to put
him to rest. Borne

into the surgery
on a board like a hero
carried on his shield
over a corpse-strewn field
he was laid on a narrow
strip of leathery
grey canvas. A sharp
jab into the neck fur
and he began to snore.
Did a harp

play while he slept?
The handsome
young vet
knowing how a pet
must always come
to such an end, wept
all the same.
We left with no more
than the collar-tag that bore
his number and name.

Beyond Posterity

My aunt, the architect,
left monuments to herself
throughout the district
where we lived, a wealth

of great houses, a school,
the church. Could she achieve
immortality through the cool
distinctive

form of each brick-built structure?
You'd assume a house would outlast
words on paper, or a picture;
in the past

that was the case, of course:
the buildings preserved for the future's eye,
the monasteries and forts
on the bone-dry

hilltops of Spain, the relics
in Rome and Palmyra,
have survived to awe and perplex
tourist and terror

group alike over centuries.
Yet as I went
down the street on one of those days
of pleasant

autumnal sunlight, and passed
a house the local guide
attributes to my aunt, I noticed
it had been destroyed;

a heap of broken stone
was all that remained
of the archways and mezzanine
levels, the shuttered

windows in the asymmetric
façade; all of my aunt's
creation was reduced to brick
dust and bent

metal fragments as fragile,
after all, as a sheet
of paper, or a pile
of ashes. The street

would not be the same.
Within a matter of weeks
a featureless box had come
to take the place of my aunt's unique

design. More such boxes had grown
nearby. How long would it be
before the church was gone
beyond posterity?

Dry Rot

Making conversation while waiting on the tee
I mentioned that I'd been in hospital
with a faulty heart. "Is that all?"
said one of the others. "I am having chemotherapy
for prostate cancer." "Well, I have got
leukemia," said another. The third
member of the foursome didn't utter a word,
so we turned to him. "I would not
go to the doctor. I don't want to find out
what is wrong with me," he said.
We each hit a ball into the familiar
green landscape that appeared before us, regular
in its contours as a flowerbed,
a tree-framed vista that survived the spring drought.

Leukemia. It was a threat that loomed
over us all, like the creaking, dry-rot-riddled tree limb
above the second tee. It was not only him
who felt its presence: everyone assumed
the disease would return from the remission
that allowed our friend to be on the course,
and that when it did it would be worse.
Playing in a golf competition
distracted him, but there would be times
when he would mention a detail

of his treatment, the weekly blood tests
and plasma transfusions, the sickening side effects,
the wait for transplants that might fail,
the hormones and enzymes.

When our friend did not play, we all feared
what his absence might mean – the return
of the adversary within, discerned
in a low blood-count, so, being men, we jeered
and joked about it, trying to lighten
the burden each of us felt. A joke
may not be amusing, but it broke
the tension that otherwise would tighten
with each message that explained
another absence. For weeks he was not there.
The limb with dry rot broke, and fell
onto the tee. Greens sloped as if an ocean swell
rose under them. White orbs soared into the air.
He had never complained.

Part Four

HALLUCINATIONS

The Stuffed Crocodile

The stuffed crocodile in the Darwin museum
is the size of an automobile, one able
to carry two rows of passengers, and it is
armour-plated, equipped with dagger-shaped teeth,
and yet in its lifetime it was known by an amiable
nickname, as if it were some
kindly uncle and not a monster that was
known to attack fishermen in their boats. In death

it is preserved in all its awe-inspiring bulk,
along with birds and lizards, and souvenirs
of the cyclone that swept the whole city away.
Most of Darwin, now, is new, as if purpose-built
for a film set – hotels with gleaming veneers
that overlook deep waters concealing the hulks
of vessels sunk in air-raids. The day
that war arrived in this small town, and spilt

bombs like terrible hailstones onto wooden shacks
and anchored ships, is a day that has another
museum dedicated to it. At the time
most of the country was prevented from knowing
of the air-raids. In the Botanic Gardens vines smother
the trunks of exotic trees, and winding tracks
climb a hillside under ferns, green slime
on creek bed stones. There are young people glowing

with health on the streets and in the cafes, joking
and calling out to one another, for this city
is made for the young, with their bright clothes and manner
of careless self-love. It is no place for old
men, a country surrounded by a pure blue sea.
The purity is misleading. Beneath its blueness, snaking
in the tide-drawn currents like football club banners,
are the poisonous box jellyfish, where the cold

depths of those waters only seems inviting.
In the car park above each curving white sand beach
a warning sign advises *Crocodiles*
inhabit this area. They will notice you
before you notice them. The angry slurred speech
of the long-grassers, sprawled out or fighting
in the casuarina shade; the vacant miles
of woodland beyond the shopping malls and mango

farms of the city limits. Within that woodland
one finds immense termite mounds marching through the trees
like an army of silent robots – or else they
could be ruins of a vanished civilisation,
pillars and crumbling towers brought to their knees
by the ages, monuments left in the sand.
The heat is unchanged from day to day,
and the fierce sun drops into the shining ocean.

What About the Groom?

The bridal party crowds the dressing room
with bouquets, food and patterned drapes.
But does anybody think about the groom?

Jewels, fabrics, over-priced perfume,
bowls of pineapples and grapes:
the bridal party crowds the dressing room.

Condemned, he stands before impending doom,
a prisoner with no means of escape:
has anybody thought about the groom?

Perfect bliss, we happily assume,
is present in its most idealised shape
among the party in the dressing room.

The bride is an exotic flower in bloom.
Held together with string and masking tape,
does anybody think about the groom?

A wedding is an antidote for gloom,
a remedy for bruises, scars and scrapes.
The bridal party crowds the dressing room.
Has anybody thought about the groom?

The Hand of God

The building site crane arches high over the highway like a footbridge.
A full-rigged

sailing ship could pass beneath it. Cement mixing trucks pause
in its shadows

- hatched and striped – with drums revolving slowly
like a ball idly

spun from hand to hand, or like the chambers
of a revolver

in a game of Russian Roulette. Wearing luminous jackets
and white helmets

workmen swarm over the scaffolding as ants clamber
all over

an animal's corpse. At ground level, on a public road,
there are dead-eyed

young women holding up paddles to advise us STOP or SLOW.
It looks somehow

as if the crane's extended beam is being held out toward
a second

crane on a neighbouring building plot, reaching
as on the Sistine ceiling

the hand of God stretches toward a new creation
that is a naked man.

Tinnitus

The hum of a powerful engine idling
among the trees;
but when one looks up at the light
thousands of bees

are swarming, a galaxy of dark stars,
making their sound
in unison as they swirl and orbit
above the ground,

before, also in unison, they return
to their hive,
a fungus-like growth on a tree-fork.
The bees live

like humans in an apartment building
side by side
in furnished comfortable cells
well supplied

with warmth and nourishment, and drones
set out each day
to perform the tasks assigned to them
where flowers sway

in the breeze. They hover like anxious parents
over each petal
loaded with pollen, before choosing one
to settle

on, then become like window cleaners attached
to a high-rise
office tower – and those structures resemble a hive,
though of a size

and form less natural and organic
than these bags
slung over the bare stripped shoulders of ghost gums.
Discarded rags

on the ground are sheets of bark fallen
from the trees,
while deep in the earth the ants work to build
their cities.

Like tinnitus, the sound that the bees make seems
to linger
after it has gone, a sound hard to place
one's finger

on, like the buzz one absorbs when close to an electric
power line
or like a bathroom fan's half-heard, half-silent
constant whine.

The Electric Didgeridoo

Riverbeds, twisted
as the unkempt hair
of a homeless person,

and framed by an aircraft
porthole, form patterns
where they meet

the sand dunes
that are the colour
of a peeled

sweet potato, and break
like waves against
other dunes,

on a vast
waterless coast.
Those patterns

bring to mind
the paintings
that humans devised

to describe themselves
once to strangers
coming on ships,

and those painters
left descendants
who have

continued to use
the methods
passed down

through the ages,
the dabs and points
and lines

that echo the forms
one can see
from the air.

The land beneath
our plane is vaster
than Europe,

and arid
as a scene
in the Bible,

yet people
adapted to it
without the need

for roads and buildings,
and instead of towns
they created

art that has survived
countless centuries.
Now a group

of artists
from the Territory
have been flown

to a city
art museum
to talk about

traditional practice:
their explanation
of the spiritual

content
of works that seem
no more than

abstract designs
resonates
as we learn

that every brush stroke
is loaded
with meaning,

referring to myths, taboos
and totems
that are as real

to them as the modern
world. Then they turn
from those mythologies

to Ipads and mobile phones
that they are
as grateful for

as for their houses
and four-wheel drives,
and send out

messages
as deep as
the songlines.

A heritage
of living stones
and animals

that spoke
is present
to us all

as we listen
to the tones
filling the room

emitted from
an amplified
electric didgeridoo.

Grandfathers

Blue Tongue Joe

Only one of my grandfathers survived
into my own lifetime, the one on my mother's side.
He was a soft-spoken gentleman with eyes

that crinkled humorously, and a hairless skull.
When we met he would always ask me to tell
him whether I had seen a steamroller:

it was a joke that I did not understand.
He lived in a white roughcast weatherboard
house that had shady wide verandahs and

a garden where lawns and vegetable
plots led to a row of conifers, tall
to a child's vision as a nursery rhyme hill.

His diet comprised nothing but meat
and potatoes, and he was never unwell, at least
not until, as a very old man, he went

to bed for a week, at the end of which he died.
He had joined the Royal Navy when aged
just twelve, and rose through the rigid

seniority system until he was
an admiral. He took me for a walk, once,
down the steeply sloping street outside his house,

before turning into a laneway
that led between a picket fence and a rockery
garden of rounded boulders, an array

forming a pattern not unlike reptilian
scales. There, peering out from behind a stone,
polished and smooth as an onion,

was a lipless mouth and eyes glassy as beads
on a torso thick as one's forearm – it was a lizard
posted like a uniformed guard.

My grandfather stopped. He seemed to know
the lizard. "That is my friend," he said. Who
could guess? "His name is Blue Tongue Joe."

Black medicine

The morning after her hundredth birthday party
my mother perches on a chair in her room
at the nursing home, and talks as she always

has, without interruption. When the Nigerian
male nurse comes to the door to offer her lunch
she sends him away. Her recollection

takes her back to the nineteen twenties
while outside the building midsummer
heat shimmers over a green expanse

where voices are calling and figures dressed
in white stand still and then move. To take in
that grassy vista one has to enter a code

into a keypad at the door – my mother's home
resembles a prison where the innocent are held
against their will, or at least from where some

would escape if they were able, for old age
itself is a prison. She can remember being alive
in simpler days, and the details of a voyage

around the world to meet her father's father,
an Irish doctor in Portrush. His practice
was well known in the town, where he would offer

his patients a choice: The Black Medicine
or The White Medicine (one assumes that meant
Guinness or whiskey, unless the line

referred to cod liver oil and milk
of magnesia). When my mother landed
in Ireland, her grandfather said he would take

her with him to visit a patient in a village
over the border in the republic – to get
to the south, they had to drive north to the edge

of the territory ruled by the British. A guard
peered out from a sentry box at the border,
and questioned my mother's grandfather, who said

"I'm going to see an old man in that village over
there." The sentry waved the car through,
and at a house nearby my mother

waited outside. Her grandfather returned
to the car, and drove back to the border.
The same guard greeted them: "How'd

you get on with old man?" he asked.
"I killed him," said the doctor.
"You did well," said the guard.

The Rainbow Funeral

We left town under clear sky, heading north.
The highway straddled a broad tidal river
with its islands and oyster farms, pleasure
boats and rock faces like cloud forms, all worth
stopping for on another day, before
we climbed inland to be flanked by tight-packed
tree plantings that were stacked
dense as hedges. On this day, to be the driver

felt like a privilege, as scenery
glimpsed sideways through the screen was cancelled
by speed. Two hours on the road, then the car
parked on a verge opposite to a country
church. A crowd of strangers stood outside, unsure
of what to say to one another. Faint
music emerged through the door, so we went
in to find a pew. Before the altar, held

up on wheels and smothered in fresh flowers,
the coffin. Inside it, a familiar
form, almost unbearable to think about,
no longer at that kitchen table of ours
reading and spilling his tea, talking out
his latest concern. The sky that was clear
when we entered the church, as bright and clean
as glass, darkened over the camellia

trees that lined the roadside. As the service
progressed there came a tumbling sound
as if the coffin's occupant had turned
over in his sleep, so some were nervous
that he might be resurrected, and
return to walk among us – but it came
from a thunderstorm outside, and the rain
rushed over the stony consecrated ground.

The wooden box was borne along the aisle
by six strong men. Everyone followed,
and organ music played. The box settled
in the rear of a station wagon while
the crowd looked on in the cloud-mottled
light – and then the vehicle rolled away
behind three priests with their grey
hair and their white robes, walking slowly on the road.

At last we returned to the country road
that had led this way, driving past a file
of trees and farm buildings, crops and bales of hay,
slopes and rivulets. Then suddenly there glowed
above the earth, and above the day,
an ordinary rainbow, as if to stand
for he who had departed. It was there to hand
us back to our ongoing lives in literary style,

as a knowing textual reference, its arc lighting
up the land his written words once imbued
with depth and meaning, the trees
and animals and humans fighting
for survival against the elements. Past milk factories,
pine plantations, dams and inlets,
cars were racing on the highway like bullets,
while cattle waited on fields the rain renewed.

Parkland Imagism

A cyclist's reflection
speeding
in a long rain puddle.

*

A mynah bird picking among
fresh horse droppings,
with the air of a civil servant
turning over an official form.

*

From depths of shadow
you notice sunlight
on distant buildings.

*

Winter-bare willow branches
like wicker baskets.

*

Roots of the Moreton Bay fig tree
dangling like tails
of cattle.

*

Coming over the hill,
a glimpse of the harbour.

*

A path among the trees
that resembles
a mouldy carpet.

*

A wind gust blows up a cloud
of dust, and a woman
seems to materialise out of it.

*

A fallen palm frond
curled up like a snail.

*

In the avenue of fig trees
mounted police in procession
wearing dark rain-capes.

*

The city's graph-shapes
half-erased
by mist.

*

Leafless poplars
like the framework
of an unfinished building.

*

Distant office towers loom
suddenly, the way a mountain peak
appears at the head of a river valley.

*

The conversation of ducks
on the lake, like a foul-mouthed
bar-room argument.

*

A wagtail seems
to be dressed
in a dinner suit.

*

An empty sky: beneath it
the office buildings
look like broomsticks
propped against a newly painted wall.

*

Naked eucalypt limbs
as pleasing to the eye
as the unclothed human form.

*

Debris like tide wrack
after a night
of thunderstorms.

*

Green moss
on a shady brick wall.

*

After high wind
lopped branches are scattered
as if left
by pruning.

*

A fir tree
shaped like a pipecleaner.

*

Tall buildings
seen over water.

*

The lake's surface
matted with weed
like a tapestry.

*

Two girls with ponytails
riding horses whose tails
match those of their riders.

*

A cockatoo in a field
like a sheet of paper.

*

A dead bird's feathers
spread out like broken glass
after a car accident.

*

A wall is being
painted olive green
by a man
high up a ladder.

*

Every grass blade is shining
after the rain;
in the distance
the sound of one dog barking.

Dementia Test

A fine mind reduced by the years
to confusion submits to diagnostic tests.
Presented with random lists
of names, this kindly, genial man has few ideas

as to who the listed people might once
have been, figures from history
or his oldest friends – all are a mystery,
meaningless as empty store fronts,

until he comes to one. "Adolf Hitler?"
he wonders. "Do I know him?"
Life with dementia suddenly seems less grim.
Hitler might have been a forgotten neighbour,

and the whole world may never
have been, on that account, at war.
He smiles from his wheelchair
as if he has said something clever.

Incognito

Is this a science fiction
setting, where faceless robots
swarm the streets?

The population goes incognito
in masks, like the old-time bank robbers
who threatened the tellers with a pistol,

though this is an age where robberies
are carried out by phone
or through the computer.

The queue at the supermarket
could be taken for a surgical team
prepared for an operation.

At the masked ball
no-one reveals their identity
before going home.

Thieves burst into a convenience
store, wearing the government's
compulsory personal protection.

Who was that masked man?
the grateful citizens asked, as the anonymous
crime-fighter rode out of town.

Welders, industrial cleaners,
murderous terrorists, protestors
ashamed of their principles –

all of these might now be mistaken
for everyday shoppers
in the crowded malls

where money changes hands
as it always has, while everywhere
we are muzzled like animals.

Cloud Land Imagism

Clouds like lookout towers
seen over an open meadow.

*

The smoke from a factory
like a stack of plates.

*

A white car parked
between two lakes, and geese
on the water beside it.

*

Apartment buildings
like the walls
of a prison.

*

A rain cloud
the colour
of anger.

*

Tassels of rain hang
out of a cloud, like the fringe
of a Persian rug.

*

Clouds on the horizon like the high white hats
worn by fashionable women at a race meeting,
while others resemble the cream cakes and meringues
in the refreshment tent at the same event.

*

Clouds like the piled-up shorn fleece
on the floor of a shearing shed.

*

Ridges and spurs and hilltops of cloud
looking like the coast of another country.

*

Cloud like a vast stone-littered desert.

*

Dark mountainous clouds,
their high peaks gilded
by the rising sun.

*

A sky of oddly artificial clouds,
resembling dishes and fluffy balls,
brick pathways and shelves,
seeming remnants
of a cosmic garage sale.

*

A series of figurative clouds –
a quiff of hair, with a few loose strands;
a corkscrew and a saw, or the beak
of a sawfish;
a row of stepping stones.

*

The first day of spring:
black cloud mountains,
so high they have wreaths
of smaller clouds wound
about their summits.

*

Grey sky
pressed down
like a saucepan lid.

*

White clouds skim like yachts
above the deep blue water
of the estuary:
their shadows overtake
the heeling yachts.

Hallucinations

Cobwebs like fine electric cables, strung
from tree to tree –

how often have hair and lips and hands
become entangled

in these filaments, adhesive and invisible,
as one struggled

through the garden gate? Yet aglow with dew
they might be

jewel-bright artefacts of a distant
civilisation,

or else the street plan of its capital.
The webs work

like fish nets, harvesting insect protein
in the dark,

but when they have been destroyed
by some conflagration

or mishap their architects rebuild
with delicate

limbs that re-shape the complex designs
reminding us

of curtains, drapes and tapestries
in the dust

of the shed, or wedding veils
and intricate

visions in the corners of verandahs,
visions

like the hallucinations experienced
from the bed

of a nursing home by a century old
woman who

tells her carers of a fire burning in her room,
adding, "You

must see the flames. I've called
the fire brigade,"

before going on to wonder why
the smoke

seems "strange and fine, like spider webs,
or airmen's overcoats."

Part Five

ORPHANS AND PRINCES

Note

At the end of the past millennium, a newspaper, *The Australian*, invited Dr David Christian, a lecturer in History at Macquarie University, to compile a list of the twenty-five historical figures who had done the most to influence the course of the twentieth century without having lived in that century. Reading about the lives of those influential figures, I learned that as many of them had been the privileged offspring of rulers or aristocrats as had been orphans who triumphed over early adversity. The poems that follow are versified biographies of those twenty-five famous personages. The verse forms employed are, from time to time, intentionally borrowed from other well-known poems.

Magnanimity

Raised by a herdsman after the King of the Medes,
who was his mother's father, had a dream
about his own overthrow, the story of Cyrus reads
more like myth than history; it would seem
to resemble the Bible's account of Moses,
or the legend of Rome's foundation.
He was probably born in Persis,
a province of what we now call Iran,
and he returned there when he was old enough
to fend off his enemies. The first of his conquests
was his grandfather, which would appear to prove
that the future, once foreseen, cannot be changed, lest
it be thought possible: the prophecies
in legends are always fulfilled, despite
the attempts of Herod or Oedipus
to avert them. It is futile to fight
against one's fate. Having thus defeated
the Medes, Cyrus inherited their empire,
after which his power consolidated
when he marched against Croesus, an entire
triumph that brought him both the wealth that king
was fabled for, and all the Greek cities
on the Aegean Sea as his subjects. Next thing,
he turned to Babylon, antiquity's
greatest power. When he had come to succeed

in the capture of that capital his rule
was tolerant and wise. The Jews were freed
from slavery by Cyrus, according to the Bible,
and allowed to return to their homeland.
He conciliated those he had conquered,
and formed alliances among a diverse band
of Asia Minor's rulers; he preferred
the use of diplomacy to force of arms
as a means of creating what became
the greatest empire of his time. Farms
and cities prospered under his laws. His fame
was to inspire Alexander the Great, who learned
about him in Herodotus, the Greek
historian. The reputation he earned
was as one who was kind-hearted yet not weak,
magnanimous and daring. His conduct
continues to have an influence, even
today, on theories of leadership. Sucked
toward him by a draught of fate, a woman
brought about his death. She had long since sworn
revenge after he had captured
her son in battle, the unforgiving queen
of a tribe of nomads from the Caspian
Sea. Thus all his magnanimity
could not save him. He had anointed his son,
Cambyses, as his successor, but the mighty
empire soon declined, the Persian throne
being seized by a usurper who had posed

as the new emperor's murdered brother. The true
ruler, meanwhile, had given himself up to what was supposed
to be a life of drunkenness and cruelty so
hideous it could scarcely
be conceived. In short, Cyrus, despite
all his great qualities, had left a legacy
his heirs would squander as if it were their right.

Transience

Not much is agreed for certain about
Siddhatta Gotama, who was the son
of a ruler in the foothills of Nepal. Doubt
even attaches to the time of his birth, one
school of belief making it more than a
century before the other. His life
story is redolent of the manner
fairytales begin with, from the young wife
who was his cousin to the luxury
of his upbringing. Yet when his own son
was born he fled: leaving the princely
life behind, he set out to find a Brahman
who could give him enlightenment. The truth
eluded him for six long years, even though
he starved himself until with every tooth
loose in his jawbone he could scarcely go
further in his self-mortification,
his limbs like withered creepers with knotted
joints. When he came to the realisation
that such austerity had defeated
its purpose he began to eat again,
a normal diet. After those six years
he was determined, still, to attain
enlightenment, and thus on one of the Kashmir's
warm evenings he sat down at the base

of a mythically-named Bo tree,
having decided that he would not rise
until in possession of the knowledge which he
had sought so long. Deep in meditation,
he remained unmoving throughout the night,
until with the new day's exhalation
he arrived at that level of insight
that is called the Awakening, at the age
of thirty-five. The name he is referred
to by most often – "The Buddha" – means "The Sage"
or "The Enlightened One". Spreading the word
of his discovery, he devoted
the rest of his life to preaching. Disciples
flocked after him, and he soon promoted
monastic orders all over India, from the hills
to the hot plains. Even his abandoned
son became one of those who would follow
him throughout the land, to be enlightened
by The Buddha's wisdom. Like a swallow,
he migrated from place to place, charming
everyone he met with his presence,
which was said to be noble and disarming,
while his complexion was the essence
of beauty. Only after forty-five
years did he feel that his mission had reached
fulfilment, and that he had no more to live
for: on a couch between two trees, he preached
one final time, saying, "Transient are all

conditioned things. Try to accomplish
your aim with diligence." Just as a wall
of stone will end in dust, and the anguish
of every age will fade as do bright
pigments exposed to sunshine, his body
began to exchange molecules for light
in the witness of his followers. He
had made transience the core of his thought,
along with the conviction that matter
is always in a state of flux, a hard-fought
revelation arrived at in a latter
form, after more than two millenniums,
by Sir Isaac Newton. Centuries more
have passed, and beneath the prosceniums
of dark-filled cinemas many an actor
who lights up the screen professes a faith
in The Buddha, as do shiftless figures
on drug-hazed communes, searchers for the path
to wisdom, and saffron-robed monks whose rigours
and rituals impress us even though
they must have known many mutations since
being devised such a long time ago
by a heartless, child-neglecting, handsome prince.

Exile

K'ung Ch'in became known as K'ung-fu-tzu,
which translates as Master K'ung, only by
the time he was in his thirties; those who
live in the West at first used to try
rendering that sequence of alien sounds
with the Latin transcription "Confucius".
There were dukes and princes to be found
in his lineage, but it seemed inauspicious
when his father died young, while K'ung was only
a three-year-old. The orphan's early life
was haunted by the prospect of poverty,
but the court would not allow the surviving wife
of one with such connections to sink to the depths
that yawned, and her son was soon employed
by the government, behind a stone desk,
as manager of the stables; he enjoyed
promotion when hired to keep the books
in a granary, and for all this time
he was studying, absorbing what it took
to master the six arts, from the sublime
subtleties of ancient Chinese ritual
to archery, charioteering, music,
calligraphy and arithmetic. When all
of that was within his grasp he was quick
aged only twenty to begin to teach

others, and was the first Chinese master who sought
to make education possible for each
and every man. For years, while he taught,
his reputation rose: the duke of Lu
thought well enough of his abilities
to appoint him governor of Chung-tu,
and later to various ministries,
including that of justice and crime.
He travelled with the duke on diplomatic
missions, and for the people his time
as a magistrate saw a dramatic
reformation of public manners. Yet
such was his moral propriety
that he began to feel unable to accept
the indulgence and sensuality
of the duke's court, so he departed
from the country aged in his late fifties
accompanied by a growing , assorted
band of students and followers. The countries
and states he visited during his exile,
which lasted a dozen years, were many.
He developed a philosophical style,
and grew ever more famous. His enemy
died, and a new duke welcomed him, but
he did not return to government.
Instead, in his last years he tried to put
into order the precise lineament
of his ideas, teaching and writing,

and working to restore the classical
traditions of Chinese culture. Citing
the Confucian "golden rule" may be all
that most can remember of his thought
in the West, but his influence remains
profound among his countrymen, who have caught
from the Confucian Analects a humane
morality without a religious
dimension. Still, after he died, aged
in his seventies, his illustrious
life complete, and all his desires assuaged,
a ruler commanded that a temple
be built where sacrifices were offered
to the spirit of the sage – a simple
contradiction of his teaching. Deferred
to and admired in his life, he had no wish
for deity, and neither denied nor slighted Heaven.
In the temple grounds, the brimming goldfish
ponds soothe the monks, with their heads new-shaven.

History

History begins with the first historian,
but little is known about the personal
history of Herodotus, the founder
of that genre which aims to shape the way
we think about the past. He was, it seems,
born somewhere in Asia Minor, and may
have lived in Athens at around the time
Sophocles was there: he is thought to have
met the great tragedian. And he might
then have moved to an Athenian
colony in Southern Italy, before
setting out on travels which would take him
over much of what the Greeks knew the world
to contain, from Egypt to the Black Sea.
He saw both the River Danube and the Don,
and in every place he journeyed to
he gathered material for the book
which was to exceed in fame the life
of its author. He wrote about the wars
between Greece and Persia, which ended not long
before his presumed time of birth; he sought
to explain not just the course of war
but its causes as well. That should still be
history's purpose now, though there are not
a few who prefer to study the past

through a refracting lens, one which will
magnify a certain thesis. The truth
ought to be able to defy such
refractions, though we cannot guess the future
and its theorists. Above all, Herodotus
was a story-teller: his history
is rich with anecdote concerning all
the prominent figures from the ages
he depicts, digressing skilfully. Truth,
for him, was an artist's truth, and he honed
dialogue so that each story would read
convincingly as narrative; the work
is an artistic masterpiece. How long
did he live? We cannot know. He must still
have been living when the latest event
alluded to by him took place; whether
he died soon after, or survived for more
than a decade, is of no importance,
for a work of art transcends the mundane
life of its creator. History
survived him, to become both a method
and a discipline, as well as an art
form; it can be a tool for oppressors
or liberators, depending on who
wields it; in honest hands it remains
an honest implement, a mattock, spade,
or plough, uncovering the long-buried
footprints of those who went before; others,

though, leave salient matter still concealed,
and blur the sequence, so that those
prints appear to have taken a direction
they never really could. Nonetheless
Herodotus knew that the truth about
our past must inform the present; he sought
to present that truth in a form that all
could understand, and that all could remember.
Now history ends with us, and begins
again when we are under the wind-driven sands.

Teacher

Aristotle had spindly legs, and eyes
which were too small, while his voice was weak
and affected by a lisp he'd disguise,
while he dressed notably well. His physique
did not affect his studies, though; he learned
medicine from his father, who was court
physician to the king, and the unearned
connection with royalty meant his thought
gained recognition from the first. He went
from Macedonia, aged just eighteen,
to Athens and that great establishment,
the Academy of Plato. A keen
student, he stayed for all of two decades,
thinking and teaching, until Plato died.
At first he lingered in the cool arcades
and libraries of Athens; to decide
his next move, Philip, King of Macedon,
asked him to return and act as tutor
to young Alexander, his teenage son.
Philip's first child would in the near future
be known to legend as Alexander
the Great. Aristotle trained the boy
in every branch of knowledge, and a
most attentive pupil he proved. What joy
he had in learning, though, was brief, as death

was stalking King Philip on the stony road
to Byzantium. In his twentieth
year, Aristotle's student bestrode
the throne which would enable him to conquer
all that he and his teacher knew the world
to be, from Egypt and Asia Minor
as far as India. A white mist swirled
over the Hellespont as the fifty-
year-old philosopher returned to live
in Athens. While his former protégé
marched through Palestine, he started to give
lessons at a new school, the Lyceum;
Alexander overthrew the Persians, while
Aristotle walked from his gymnasium
through the gardens and the temple. A file
of students were listening while he spoke
and walked, so that the group came to be known
as the Peripatetics. Perhaps as a stroke
of misfortune, he wrote nothing down,
and thus his thought only survives in the form
of lecture notes, yet his work pioneered
what we know now as almost every arm
of learning, from literary theory
to zoology and physics. Because
he insisted on theories receiving
credence only when proved by facts, he was
the founder of modern science, believing
observations should always be preferred

to assumptions. He had married a niece
of the King of Lesbos, before the word
"lesbian" changed its meaning; but the peace
he had known was brought to an end with the death
of Alexander. He then retreated
to his mother's estates, where soon his health
declined and his life-span was completed.
Yet even after all these centuries
when conversations turn around the mind
and argument over other theories
has been exhausted, people still find
that of all authorities his is the name
they return to so as to clinch their case.
Aristotle thus earned a kind of fame
that endures as long as the human race.

Hubris

When Chao Cheng was born, his father was held
hostage in the neighbouring state of Chao,
but that was not to orphan him: skilled

at diplomacy, the father turned out to know
the official channels that would achieve
his release, and then he rose to the throne, somehow,

in the state of Ch'in – a throne he would leave
to his son when Cheng was only thirteen.
Until the young king matured enough to perceive

the extent of his duties, a regent, lean
and cunning, called Lu Pu-wei, had control
of his government. Cheng's mother had been

Lu's concubine before her marriage, a role
which ensured that Cheng's first action as king
was to send Lu into exile. The whole

of China, then, comprised six states, fighting
each other constantly, all bitterly
rivalrous: Cheng set about defeating

them, one by one, until his utterly
ruthless methods united all six under
the rule of the Ch'in. Using bribery,

espionage and torture to sunder
all opponents, and supported throughout
by gifted generals, it was little wonder

that Cheng achieved supremacy; all doubt
had been dissolved by the time he proclaimed
himself "First Sovereign Emperor of Ch'in", out

of the same hubris from which he had claimed
his dynasty would survive ten thousand
generations. Yet he could not be blamed

for such arrogance: the reforms he planned
to administer throughout his empire
brought peace and stability to the land,

such as few rulers could have, and fewer aspire
to. There would be no more lasting monument,
though, than the Great Wall guarding the entire

northern frontier of his lands, meant
to deter the threat of Mongol raids,
which he completed. Its masonry, cement

and gabled watch-towers which were to take decades
to construct with the use of slave labour, has survived
for two millenniums: climbing steep grades

and descending into valleys, it writhed
for thousands of miles across a landscape
of stony hillsides, until at last it arrived

in the twentieth century, to hang like a drape
among posters exhorting the revolt
of the masses. There would be no escape

for those masses, under Cheng, from the hold
of his police and censors: he pioneered
the totalitarian state with cold

efficiency. Yet, as time passed, Cheng feared
mortality, and became obsessed
with alchemy and magic, and a weird

search for the elixir of youth. The quest
was unsuccessful, and he was only
in his fifties when death reached him as he passed

through the outlying provinces, hardly
the age of an immortal. Within four
more years the all-powerful dynasty

had collapsed, folded upon itself, hour
by hour, like the paper fans which flourished
in the delicate hands of emperor

and concubine alike, in that long-banished
court, that almost unimaginable world
from which all but the Great Wall has vanished.

Remorse

Asoka was a prince before he rose to be
Emperor, in the Mauryan dynasty

of India; eight years into his reign
his conquest of the Kalinga region

caused such terrible loss of human blood,
and suffering among the dust and mud,

for those he had defeated, that he was
moved to deep remorse. He decided, thus,

to renounce the practice of armed conquest
henceforth: instead, he concluded, it was best

to reason with people. He converted
to Buddhism, which had been a neglected

little-known sect until then, and he commenced
a policy that he would call "conquest

by dharma". What he meant by this comprised
adherence to honesty, and to undisguised

compassion, refusing all violence
and acquisitiveness, accepting silence,

taking care not to harm any animal.
He began to make tours among the rural

people, preaching to them and relieving
their poverty and suffering,

and he appointed a special class of "dharma
ministers" to encourage similar

work among the public. He had respect
for every other religious sect.

Asoka founded hospitals, and supplied
them with medicines, and he built roadside

watering sheds and rest-houses as much
for the poor as for all travellers. Such

groves of planted trees, shelters, and temples
which he constructed, some with samples

of his sayings inscribed on them, are all
that survive him: words carved on a stone wall.

His regime was the earliest version
of the modern welfare state, and his vision

spread throughout India and beyond
its frontiers. The only glory he yearned

for, he would say, was that of having led
his people along the path of dharma. Dead

at last, having fulfilled that aim, the gift
of Asoka to his people was not left

for long: within a few years, his empire
disintegrated. The funeral pyre

would consume his bodily remains,
while his successors would take pains

to destroy all that had grown from his remorse,
making blood once again the only recourse.

Humility

Leaving out the question of paternity,
and the angels in the sky, and the kings
bearing gifts who were summoned from on high,
most of the essential things
about the biography of Jesus Christ
persuade one of their authenticity
because of the particulars which just
ring true: the census, the bureaucracy,
the hotels unable to make a booking,
the stable with its wooden feeding-trough
improvised as a cot. Anyone looking
for hierarchy should be put off
by the modesty of his background,
which is also what underlies his message.
He did not have the connections to found
a dynasty, or to expect homage
for any quality apart from his word:
other prophets and preachers had once been
warriors or princes, but he made himself heard,
even as a child, by the simple means
of personal magnetism. A refugee
soon after his birth, we have not been told
much more about his childhood, or of how he
returned from Egypt to Israel, nor how old
he was at the time; but what has survived

of him is the gist of his teaching,
which began at some point after he arrived
in the Galilean countryside, preaching
to all who would listen. He did not seem to be
a prophet or an ascetic, but instead
he worked among people in their ordinary
lives, speaking in the open air; he led
his disciples along the salt-white shore
of the lake, and spoke in the synagogues
as well as on roads and hillsides. He saw
fishermen working and farmers with their pigs,
attended weddings and spoke to the tax
collectors and the money-lenders,
and in his sermons he drew on the facts
of everyday life; the road-menders
and carpenters and small children could grasp,
hearing his words, the meaning contained
in those parables and metaphors, and gasp
if he seemed to perform miracles. That he gained
a following is beyond all the doubts
of historicity, and there is also
evidence of his execution. What flouts
all reason and logical explanation, though,
is the claim that Christ was able to rise
again from his tomb; and yet to believe
the resurrection really did take place
is the keystone for all who would cleave
to Christian faith. It has been in his name

that the greatest of all forms of culture
have arisen, though greatness was never the aim
of his ministry: he would, instead, refer
to the importance of humility,
meekness and charity. He said that love
should outweigh the legal authority
of the temple and its rabbis, and urged us above
all else to be as kind to a neighbour
as to those whose brutality we forgive
by turning the opposite side of our
slapped face. How few have been able to live
up to those precepts! In his recorded speech,
armed conquest and political power
are never enjoined on his followers: each
of his instances implies that the weak shall tower
above the strong only when last reckonings
are made. When he came to Jerusalem,
though, his arrest was always beckoning,
and what ensued proved that, at least to *them* –
the administrators – the movement he led
had been about politics, for the fate
he suffered was, in those times, reserved
for rebels against the Roman-ruled state.
Three days after the crucifixion, he rose
above mere earthly governance: all faith
in his divinity begins with those
who met him, after the presumed death
of his body, walking on sunlit roads

or in taverns filled with the cheerful sound
of public dining; he lifted his robes
to let the sceptic touch his fatal wound.

Messenger

Muhammed was orphaned twice by the age
of eight: born soon after his father
died, he was raised by his grandfather until the stage

when death interposed again; the favour
of bringing him up then fell upon his uncle.
Did rage against the fates burn like a fever

within him from that time? Within the tangle
of family relations, his uncle led the clan
they both belonged to, so from one angle

he could have been seen as a prince, or as a man
with connections to power, but his reality
at first was a scant livelihood tending sheep. He ran

into a rich widow while on a journey
with his uncle, and made such an impression
on the woman that he was able to escape poverty

by marriage. He took up the profession
of a merchant, using the capital
his wife controlled, a generous concession.

Though his senior by fifteen years, she was able
to bear six of his children; four daughters,
out of these, survived. Near Mecca, a hill

cave became his retreat, with still waters
and sword-like palm tree fronds nearby; away
from business, his friends and supporters,

he would go there to meditate, until one day
a vision came to him of a being
robed in majesty approaching to say:

"You are the Messenger of God." Seeing
the light, Muhammed went more frequently
to the cave, where he began hearing

messages which took the form of poetry,
each one comprising a short sentence in rhyme
that he believed to have come directly

from God. The verses were collected, in due time,
some six hundred and fifty of them, in
the Qur'an, but at first their full sublime

significance seemed to be lost, at least on
those people of Mecca who took him for
an eccentric poet or soothsayer. Sin

was prohibited in the messages which were,
he said, dictated, usury and wine
and gambling being among the score

of interdictions they proclaimed; there were fine
distinctions as to what God would permit
all true followers. Preaching, he adopted a line

hostile to the rich merchants, who saw fit
to oppose him in Mecca when his influence
expanded: it seemed there was nothing for it

but escape; Muhammed, hence,
embarked on what is called the *hijrah*,
or emigration, to a new home. Tents

and camels of a caravan, across the lava
plains and through the stony, treeless mountains,
brought him to the city of Medina

where he was given a house with fountains
and a courtyard around which would be grouped
the separate apartments he was to maintain

for each of his nine wives. He recouped
the losses he had made in Mecca, and soon
became the ruler of Medina. He swooped

like a falcon from behind the sand-dunes
to attack passing convoys of traders
from his former home, while the wailing tune

of the *muezzin* which, later, the crusaders
would hear in Jerusalem, filled the baked mud
alleys of the city; with his raiders

he returned enriched by plunder, blood
on his scimitar. He rose to power
by military means, and in the end subdued

even his enemies in Mecca. The flower
of his triumph still had a bitter scent
for the Jews in Medina, who would endure

Muhammed's persecution throughout the cent-
uries after his death. On the other hand,
his attitude to Jesus was reverent:

he considered Christ a prophet second
only to himself. He enjoyed a life
of action and sensual indulgence, and

of fierce armed conquest. At last, the strife
was over; he made a final pilgrimage
then died in the lap of his favourite wife.

Medicine

Avicenna was a doctor
by the age of twenty-one;
he had soon outgrown his teacher
and committed the Qur'an

to memory when still a child.
He taught himself, and soon he treated
rich and poor alike, who filed
reports which were repeated

until his reputation grew
and he reached a high position
with the prince who clearly knew
he was more than a physician;

he was one immersed in law,
religion, science, and the arts.
That understanding was all for
nothing, when, forced to other parts

in Persia by the overthrow
of his patron, Avicenna,
the great doctor, had to go
wandering the burnt sienna

of the desert, in the garment
of a nomad. At Hamadan
he would come to find preferment
with that city's nobleman,

and ruler, Prince Shams al-Dawlah,
by whom he was twice appointed
to the post of vizier.
Much admired and anointed,

He began to write the books
which would make his name eternal
in the circles of Islam. Rooks
built their nests upon the temple

of the hooded vizier, while
he set his system down in words.
Field mice running through the aisles
of the wheat crop, watched by birds,

were embraced within the essence
of his system, for which God
is necessary to existence.
Avicenna, with his rod

and gown and quill-nibbed pen,
worked until Prince Shams al-Dawlah
died, and then he fled again,
to find shelter with the ruler

of Isfahan. He was admired
not only for his intellect,
to which few men could have aspired,
but also for his bodily strength:

he fought for his new patron's cause
as one among the infantry,
even while devising laws.
He set out with the military

on a warlike expedition
only to fall ill with colic,
an unusual condition
for a full-grown man. Too sick

to heal himself, although he tried,
Avicenna, the great doctor,
lawyer and philosopher,
stretched out in his tent and died.

Terror

Temujin lost his father when he was nine,
and after that he lived in poverty for a time,

a nomad, on the steppes of Mongolia,
no purer or holier

than a wandering dervish or monk.
He grew up. The blood of a goat was drunk

at his wedding. Soon afterward, his young wife
was stolen and raped, and her life

held to ransom by another tribe, the Merkit:
Temujin saw his duty, and would not shirk it.

He approached the most powerful Mongol prince
of the time, to form an alliance;

together they attacked
the Merkit, and, victorious, Temujin hacked

off the heads of all the Merkit nobility,
recruiting those he spared to his soldiery.

Using this method, his power grew. He would defeat a clan,
or a nation, in battle, then every man

among his enemy who was taller than the height
of a cart-axle would be slaughtered. The fight

went out of his opponents rapidly,
faced with these tactics; systematically

he eliminated every possible rival
so that, on his arrival

at a great assembly held on the banks
of the River Onon, the gathered Mongol ranks

gave him the title Universal Ruler, or Genghis Khan.
It was the first time that one man

had led the Mongol clans and tribes
without resorting to bribes

or pleading: Genghis Khan had founded a nation,
and the explanation

for his achievement lay exclusively
in terror. Using cavalry

to defeat his fellow-nomads, he was disciplined,
mobile, and ruthlessly organised,

and soon his armies were able to lay siege
to cities, his liege

followers equipped with mangonels,
catapults, ladders, burning oils, and everything else

the technology of those years
could devise as armoury. His engineers

even knew how to divert rivers
while his troops tore out the livers

of those they had defeated. Though unable to read,
Genghis Khan learned of the need

for literacy through one of his conquests: he therefore ordered
that his achievements be recorded

in writing, and that is how
we know about him now.

By the end of his life, he had conquered
all of the land which spread

from the Pacific to the Caspian Sea;
thus his history

concerns the founding of the greatest land-bound empire
that the entire

world has known. His success was such that each state
which he went on to create

outlasted his demise; his successors
continued the expansion, becoming possessors

of a wealth which had
once been unthinkable for a poor, orphaned nomad.

Discovery

In Genova, where the olive-blue mountainsides
slide down toward the curving bay, Cristoforo
Colombo was raised by a weaver. At least, so
he said; in his account of his life, he decides
to run away to sea when aged only fourteen.
Within six years, he was involved in piracy,
and in another five he was left to the mercy
of the deep when his ship – a plundered lateen –
caught fire off the coast of Portugal. He survived
by swimming to land while clinging to an oar.
Dressed in a set of borrowed clothes, he headed for
Lisbon, where his brother was working, and arrived
styling himself Cristobal Colon. His brother
was a cartographer, and something about maps
awoke in Colombo the notion that perhaps
it might be feasible to sail to the other
side of the world – to "Cathay", as the Far East
was known – westward over the Atlantic Ocean.
There was no basis in science for this notion:
it was founded on biblical prophecies, not least
on a passage in one of the Apocrypha,
and there was an error in his calculation
which made the earth's equator only a fraction
of its real breadth. Colon was less an explorer,
then, than a confidence trickster, whose only aim

was to extract finance from a wealthy patron
for a scheme he did not expect to put into action.
First he approached the King of Portugal, whose fame
as a sponsor of innovation may have been
unjustly dimmed by his refusal, and then two dukes,
both rich and powerful, wearing horse-hair perukes,
rejected the proposal. When Colon met Queen
Isabella and King Ferdinand of Spain
beneath the minarets and Moorish porticoes
of the Alhambra, and despite the fact that those
commissioners sent out by the rulers to obtain
a report on his submission responded with
a damning conclusion (they thought Columbus vague
and incoherent), he was thought less likely to plague
them with further schemes and propositions if
his requests were met. Thus it was that, furnished
with three vessels and supplies, he was able
to embark on a journey by which the impossible
would be proved: the Santa Maria could have vanished
over the edge of the level world, but instead
they reached the Bahamas after less than three months.
The return was a triumph: the King and Queen at once
received Columbus in a scene of splendour, red
and gold tapestries on the walls, the ceremony
swelling the palace with perfume and stately tunes.
The explorer became an admiral, his fortunes
enhanced by admiration, power, and enough money
to revisit the land he had discovered.

He was appointed viceroy, and returned three times.
As a governor, he committed many crimes
and was such a tyrant that he and his brothers
were brought back to Spain from his third voyage in chains
and in disgrace. Columbus thought that he had proved
not that the earth was round, but pear-shaped. Unloved
and forgotten, he died in obscurity for all his pains.

Poetry

All the poetry written in the English
language revolves around a single place,
and its importance does not diminish
with the fact that we cannot give a face
for certain to its author. Relinquish
that uncertainty, then, and fill its space
  with the portrait of a balding actor
  who may have owned the unknown factor

we label genius. We can find the date
of William Shakespeare's baptism, but not
the time of his birth, though most estimate
it to be in the year that child got
warm holy water sprinkled on his pate.
If he went to school, he did not learn a lot
  of Latin and Greek, yet signs of learning
  are abundant in the lines still earning

the attention of listeners and readers
all over the world. Aged just eighteen
he married and had a child; this may lead us
to doubt the claims made by those who maintain
that he preferred male flesh to the breeders
of children. We know the Lord Chamberlain
  included him among a company
  of players with royal assent. Many

performances, plays and poems under
the name "Shakspeer", among other spellings,
were made in his lifetime, and the wonder
is that his output has never stopped selling
tickets. From the State theatre to the rotunda
in the park, somewhere, Hamlet is telling
  his mother that he has "that within
    that passes show", a phrase that has gone in

to the vernacular so completely
that some hearers would only recognise
it as a cliché. He called his newly
born son "Hamnet", and hence one might surmise
that play to be one he particularly
favoured, though this cannot be proved. A wise
  investor and property owner, by
    the time he came to make a will the sly

humour apparent throughout his work
saw him bequeath to his wife his "second
best bed". He died a wealthy man. The mark
of his imagination can be reckoned
to consist in the ripeness of the talk
uttered through his characters, the fecund
  inventiveness of word and phrase and trope.
  Yet something about this gives others hope:

Shakespeare was never an innovator.
He devised little on his own. The plots
of his dramas draw on the narrator
of Holinshead's *Chronicles*, though some spots
take a poet's liberties. The creator
of characters who could range from tosspots
  like John Falstaff to the towering Moor
  of Venice nonetheless achieved no more

than to clothe these figures in words, then set
them in motion within the fixed scaffold
of a borrowed structure he had to get
from the classical playwrights, a form as old
as Sophocles. He would also inherit
the rhymed and metred stanzas which hold
  together the eloquence in "The Rape
  of Lucrece" and "Venus and Adonis": shape

on the page seemed to matter to him in those
poems written when the theatres were forced
to close by the plague. His mind would not close,
in those years, even though a holocaust
of disease stalked through London. To compose
even such minor works, though, which reinforced
  his popularity despite the time,
  he still depended for a storyline

on the myths of Greece and Rome. All he brought
to the conventions of his day was a skill
with words exceeding that which might be taught
or memorised; he was, as Jonson would call
him, "Honey-tongued Shakespeare". We are all caught
up with that skill, centuries later, still;
  with Hamlet's bitter retort "words, words,
   words", our minds are raised up as if by birds.

Reason

Brought up by a cross-eyed nurse and the mother
of his mother, who had died when he was one,
Rene Descartes ever after was attracted
by cross-eyed women. At first he was not expected
to survive, as he was a sickly child, but he won
a struggle against chest disease, among other

ills, to be able to attend the Catholic school
in La Fleche before going on to study
at the Protestant university beyond
the Loire in Poitiers. He was to respond
to this education at a time of bloody
conflict within the Christian church with a cool

and shrewd dispassion, so that, departing
for the Netherlands both to undertake
the study of mathematics and to join
a regiment underwritten by the coin
of Prince Maurice of Nassau, he could make
the statement that what he was starting

to study was simply the book of the world.
He travelled all over Europe, enlisting
in the Bavarian army; one day
he sat by the barracks stove on a grey
winter's afternoon, quietly persisting
with meditation, his numbed fingers curled

about a warm beaker, when he arrived
at the systemic base for the new
set of ideas from which he would conclude
Cogito ergo sum. He had renewed
rationalism, submitting all things to
the scrutiny of reason, a process derived

from mathematics that he would apply
to every branch of thought. In these years
he had no need for concern about earning
a living: inherited wealth made learning
and scholarship his entire purpose. Ideas
such as that of God as the absolutely

Perfect Being, and of the division
between mind and body, are explored
in his *Discourse on Method*, and his fame
as a philosopher was such that he came
to be invited into the royal court
of Queen Christine of Sweden. The position

offered to him by the youthful queen
was demanding for a man in his fifties:
he was asked to rise at five every
morning to give her a philosophy
lesson – the Northern cold caused him to wheeze
and suffer – and, in addition, Christine

ordered the philosopher to compose
a comedy in five acts, as well as
a ballet in verse. With the early hours
the strain was too much for Descartes' powers
of recovery; greatcoats and umbrellas
were of no more use than a book of prose,

and he contracted a chill and died.
Unless people believe immortality
and an all-powerful God awaits
them, he had written, their unknown fates
will give them no reason for morality.
A child with a broken toy, Queen Christine cried.

Equilibrium

Isaac Newton was born after the death
of his father, and lost his mother, too,
    less than two years later;
he was raised by his grandmother, who
at first did not expect him to live, for his health
was delicate. Lincolnshire: a skater

on a frozen pond, mist rising from fens,
the plains level as a draughtsman's board,
    cottages with apple
trees in their gardens. Having recovered,
Newton went to grammar school in Grantham, and thence
to Cambridge, where he could watch light dapple

the river winding behind the college
and beneath arched stone bridges. The Blue Boar
    was the name of the inn
outside the gates of Trinity; he wore
the gown and mortarboard while absorbing knowledge
from both dons and townsmen alike. To win

medals, degrees, and fellowships he worked
hard and attended all of the classes
    required then to complete
the course. Lenses and optical glasses
were among his interests, but next he was jerked
back to Woolsthorpe when Cambridge, that great seat

of learning, was closed by the plague. Two years
at home, among the thatched roofs and orchards,
    laying foundations
for the calculus, and setting standards
previously unknown, saw Newton arrive at ideas
which would lead to the laws of gravitation

and to his *Opticks*; he was much occupied
before the university re-opened.
    Then he was elected
to the fellowship he'd already earned,
and the Lucasian professorship, inside
two more years. He hated to be rejected,

for all his success, and when he became
a member of the Royal Society
    he flew into a rage
after his first paper, when not yet thirty,
met with some minor criticism. For the same
reason he had a breakdown at the age

of thirty-five, a collapse of the nervous
system which left him unable to teach
    or write. Still, in just six
more years he was revived enough to reach
a summit of rare triumph; the profoundest service
was done for physics and mathematics

by the astronomer Halley, when he
urged his friend Newton to expand his tract
    on motion. The result
was the *Principia*, which remains in fact
the base of all modern science, and not only
Newton's masterpiece. One might think no insult

could have damaged such a man, after such
achievement, yet it was not to be long
    until his next breakdown.
Grey stone cloisters in equilibrium, the song
of choristers filling the chapel's dim nave, to touch
the soul of a university town,

birds in the hedge outside the refectory:
it was a place of such calm that Newton,
    with his friable nerves,
was prone to turn inward, where emotion
seethed like the atomic particles of his theory.
Thus it suited him to forsake the curves

and mown rectangles of the college lawns
to accept a position as warden
    of the Royal Mint,
where for the rest of his life he would broaden
his knowledge with extended investigations
of alchemy, and with work on a manuscript

about the prophecies of Daniel.
He was knighted by Queen Ann at the age
	of sixty-two, but lived
on for two more decades. In his dotage
he presided over the Royal Society, and often fell
asleep during meetings, it was observed.

By the end, he was a wealthy man, yet
he never married. He would supervise
	the Mint, and then go home
to solve mathematical theories
while twilight slanted over his window as if it
were a prism, blossom on apple-boughs like foam.

Wealth

Adam Smith was born after the early
death of his father, who had been a customs
official in a village just outside
Edinburgh. He was a gifted scholar,
and earned his first degree from Glasgow while still
in his teens; next, he travelled on horseback

to Oxford, whence he would quite soon come back
to Glasgow as a professor. Early
success brought him acquaintance with scholars
such as Hume and Watt though he was still
to publish his first book, for the customs
of that town allowed him to move alongside

such figures. Hume would be by his side
when *The Theory of Moral Sentiments* came back
from the printer, and that book was early
proof of what lay before him. Still,
his next task was to tutor a young scholar,
the Duke of Buccleuch, in one of the customs

of the age, travelling in France where customs
were a novelty for him. Taken inside
the literary salons of Paris, early
in his stay, he met writers and scholars
like Turgot, Necker and Voltaire. Back
in the village he had once come from, still

cool air in the stony lanes helped to distil
his thoughts about wealth. It was his custom
to dictate his ideas, at an early
hour, and then, with the transcript beside
him, he would rework each sentence, going back
over his theories until no scholar

could fault his reasoning. In fact scholars
to come would be studying his thought still
long after *The Wealth of Nations* pushed back
the cause of tyranny. Smith was on the side
of "perfect liberty", which was how by custom
he described free markets. Just as, early

in his life, work as a scholar would still
see him reside in the village of his early
days, he ended back in Scotland, the chief of customs.

Persistence

Not much is known about the childhood
of George Washington, except that it was spent
on a farm, and that his father was dead
by the time he was nine. Someone would invent,
later, the story in which he confessed
to his father that he had cut down a tree;
in that mythical tale he was past
being the age at which, in reality,
he was already orphaned. At twenty
he had managed to become the owner
of a farming estate where plenty
and fruitful soil led to much local honour.
He joined the provincial regiment then,
and served for six years before he resigned
with the rank of brigadier gen-
eral. By this time marriage was on his mind,
so he made Martha Dandridge his wife,
the rich widowed mother of two boys,
and settled into a contented life
as a planter. The pleasant equipoise
of his days was filled with overseeing
his landholdings, attending his church,
serving as a district burgess, and being
a justice of the peace. With a lurch,
that poise was interrupted as

the American Revolution rose
like a thundercloud. He joined the members
of the first legislature, who chose
him, in the next year, as commander-in-chief
of the revolutionary army.
In accepting the command, it was his belief
that he should not receive payment any
more than his expenses. Throughout the five
years of the War of Independence
his character kept the cause alive,
no more so than through the persistence
he showed at Valley Forge. There, he endured
a winter of starvation, deep in snow
and bitter winds, his conscience tortured
by harsh public criticism, even though
he was to be proved right. In due course,
the British were defeated, whereupon
Washington resigned his commission in the force
at a ceremony during which, solemn
and dignified, he presented an account
for his expenses, made out in neat
handwriting. Having received the amount
on his invoice, he went to his retreat
at Mount Vernon, intending to resume
life as a farmer. When the Constitution
was being framed, though, he agreed to assume
chairmanship of the Convention
which debated it. When votes were cast

for the first President of the newly
united States, the first choice of every last
elector was Washington, who duly
took up the position. For two terms
of four years each he served, methodical
in his routines, his judgement sober, firm
and cautious. He retired for the final
time at sixty-five, returning to the peace
and verdant fields of his estate. In spring
there were green shoots all through the cherry trees,
while the Potomac River was winding
beside his pastures. Summer, then winter,
came. Ice floated on the river, the hills
were dusted with snow, winds which could splinter
china surged through the hanging icicles.
Washington mounted his horse, and went
out over the snow-bright land on a long ride;
the cold proved too severe this time, and bent
over and chilled through, two days later, he died.

Horsepower

James Watt was a delicate child,
too sickly to be schooled
in the conventional way;
instead, he was forced to stay
at home and learn from his father.
Such an education was rather
important to Watt, later, as the trade
of ship-builder by which his father made
a living honed his mechanical
interests. As a mathematical
instrument maker, he worked in London,
then returned to Glasgow to open
a shop of his own
in his home town.
He married his cousin,
who bore his six children
before she died nine years into their marriage.
A steam-propelled carriage,
at this time, was still no more
than an idea, although there were
primitive steam engines
based on Thomas Newcomen's
invention. At the university
of Glasgow, where he came to be
appointed the official

instrument maker, he was able
to meet with scientists, philosophers
and scholars, and in the process
became a member of a group
for whom the microscope,
the dictionary and slide-rule
were indispensable.
While repairing one of Newcomen's steam
engines – used to work a pump – he came
on a solution for the problem
of wastage which had made them
so cumbersome: the separate
condenser meant that it
became possible for an economical
steam-powered vehicle
to be constructed.
Soon, a steam-engine would be conducted
through the streets by a man
waving a flag, and then
came the first trains on rails,
ships which could move without sails,
and the subsequent innovator
who would build on oil-fuelled motor,
leading to mass-produced cars
and aeroplanes, until the stars
themselves seemed in our reach.
Watt's greatest invention meant that each
development which followed

would lead to cities being swallowed
by motorways tangled as a nest
of serpents, and to the rest
of the world drawing in. The century
after him filled up with the history
of transport. Watt was to invent
more improvements for his engine, and would patent
the sun and planet motion,
the double engine, the expansion
principle, the parallel motion,
a smokeless furnace, and the governor.
The royalties for
all of these patents made him wealthy,
yet while he remained healthy
he continued to work in the garret
of his house – no baronet,
for he had declined an offer
from the king. He would prefer
to devise a letter-copying press,
and a machine, no less,
for copying sculptures. At last,
when he died, the past
had been transformed from a place
where humans moved at a pace
that could never outspeed
the horse; Watt took that steed
as a measure of how much power
his engines could produce, and our

world, overrun by the generations
descended from his inventions,
is unlike any world he could imagine
when he first repaired a faulty engine.

Money

A house with a red shield over its door
in the Frankfurt ghetto gave a surname
to the Rothschild family. They were poor
and devoutly Jewish, so the first aim
for young Mayer Rothschild was to become
a rabbi; when both of his parents died,
though, he had to go to work, for some
years serving as an apprentice inside
a banking house at Hanover. Returned
to Frankfurt, he became a money
changer, and about the same time he earned
the first of his children's patrimony
by dealing in ancient coins and antique
furniture. When he was given a chance
to sell coins to the Elector, a unique
opening through which Rothschild would advance
his future appeared; soon, he was appointed
financial adviser to the prince,
and once he was royally anointed
began a pattern that would ever since
be followed by his family, doing
business with reigning houses for
preference, and in the meantime fathering
many sons. It was Napoleon's war
which made the Rothschilds' fortune; with his five

sons, Mayer profited by making loans
to warring rulers who could not survive
without the funds and the precious stones
he was able to transfer from country
to country, despite national borders.
He was the first to show that money
transcends the power of all other orders
of human organisation, from kings
and princes to local councillors. Armies
could rise and fall, bridges and buildings
be raised, revolutionaries might seize
a nation's government, and yet nothing
could be done without money. Would Rothschild
have guessed what his success was to bring
in a world where the bank account filled
the place of religion in many lives?
There were two business guidelines laid down
by Rothschild, and each principle still drives
the banker who daily goes into town
in his forbidding grey suit, one being
to conduct all transactions jointly,
and the other never to aim at anything
excessive in the way of profits, partly
to compensate for risks. Although Mayer
did not outlive Napoleon, his sons
continued to raise the business higher,
until the Rothschild name belonged among the ones
which possess a folk meaning far greater

than the simple sign to which it once referred.
A century, and more decades, later,
and the red shield is not just a word
but a symbol of wealth, in a context
where riches have ceased to consist of treasure
one can ogle, become mere cybertext
and rows of numbers, from which few could know pleasure.

Rights

Mary Wollstonecraft
needed to support
herself from the age
of nineteen; she taught

and then worked as a
governess, having
been companion,
first, to a giving

generous lady.
Contact with the rich
led her to a job
translating, at which

she was proficient,
for the publisher
Johnson, and in turn
she would be a fisher

of minds, an author,
as she came to meet
writers, reformers,
and those who would treat

intellectual
subjects as something
any person could
join in. Her writing

began with a book
on the rights of man,
in which she replied
to Burke's reflection

on the recent French
revolution. Rights
were an idea,
then, fixed in the sights

of many thinkers;
thus she made the stride
to justifying
the rights of one side

of what is our
human equation.
Her major work was
the *Vindication*

of the Rights of Women,
which would foreshadow
the doctrines later
generations know

as the feminist
theory, and her
defence of women
achieves a splendour

few of those jargon
filled tracts can attain.
And yet, despite all
that, she would remain

unable to make
much of a defence
of herself, when she
fell into a dense

and passionate and
hopeless love affair
with Captain Imlay,
a seedy timber

merchant, who would leave
her after she gave
birth to his daughter.
Someone else would save

her when she made an
attempt at drowning
herself in the Thames,
over which, frowning,

she stood on Putney
Bridge. She then began
a new liaison
with William Godwin,

the philosopher,
and at last her life
seemed settled and calm.
She became his wife

after she conceived
her second daughter,
Mary, who would grow
some decades later

to achieve a fame
of her own, writing
a gothic novel
after inviting

the poet Shelley
into her life. Yet
Mary Shelley was
not destined to get

to know her mother,
who died eleven
days after the birth:
she grew up an orphan.

Emperor

At a boarding school, every pupil
   is an orphan,
even though both of their parents may still
be living; likewise, each pupil is an
only child, regardless of how many
siblings they actually have. Sent to
military school at the age of nine,
Napoloeone Buonaparte, as he
spelled his name at first, was one of those who
was thus made an only child, benign

though the intentions of his father,
   a proud, wealthy
lawyer from Corfu, may have been. Rather,
the outcome may be seen as unhealthy,
as the boy, who was also undersized,
was hurt into a hidden ambition
which would for a time change much of the world.
Aged just sixteen, he quickly realised
the first of his aims, as on graduation
he was made second lieutenant. Tight-curled

epaulettes on both shoulders attested
    to promotions
through the ranks, his rapid rise assisted
with the influence of connections
made by his father. The Revolution
began when he was twenty, and only
four years later he was a brigadier
general, the post a recognition
of his part in defeating an army
at Toulon. As year succeeded to year,

other successes in battle earned
    him popular
acclaim in Paris, so that when he learned
the government of the *Directoire*
was falling into disfavour, he left
Egypt to return to the capital.
Soon a coup d'etat installed him as one
of three consuls in power. In a deft
move, at thirty, he was master of all
France. Though propelled by the Revolution,

Bonaparte's rise owed to the qualities
    which marked him out
from his comrades in the military's
lowest ranks. Of his gifts there is no doubt.
Despite the arrival of a new
democratic century, he remained

the last of the previous age's
ideal, an enlightened despot, who
would rule with absolute force, unrestrained
by parliaments or councils and judges.

The new first consul never ceased being
     a soldier, ruled
by an orderly structure leading
from highest to lowest, with each rank schooled
in obedience to its senior.
He did not respect the sovereignty
of the people, even though they voted
for him as though he were their saviour
when he made peace with Britain three
years into his consulate. Devoted

above all to military conquest,
     he was at war
with Britain again a twelve-month at best
later, and soon crowned himself Emperor,
endorsed by the Pope, as a way, he claimed,
to discourage conspiracies and plots
against his life. Yet he could not defeat
the British navy, although cities flamed
throughout Europe as his well-drilled despot's
columns marched across the land. To complete

his triumph, he gave the thrones of each country
    he overran
to the brothers from whom, in his early
days, he had been parted. Within the span
of a decade, a Bonaparte was king
in Naples, Holland, Westphalia
and Spain, while Napoleon's three sisters
were married to princes. He could not bring
the British to accept his regalia,
though, and then a series of disasters

ensued when he sought to intimidate
    the Tsar. Moscow
in winter was deep in snow, the sky slate
grey. Troops lay dead on the roadside, as though
sculpted from ice. The *Armee*, defeated
by the Russian climate, returned to France
in a deeply humiliated state,
so that, two years after they retreated,
Napoleon's opponents saw their chance
for compelling him to abdicate.

He was exiled to an obscure island,
    Elba, between
Corsica and Italy, having signed
a treaty at Fontainebleau which would mean
that he retained his imperial
title, and still received French revenues

while keeping sovereignty only over
the island. Despite the material
comfort he enjoyed, the quiet and the views,
Napoleon was restless on Elba.

In Paris, the Bourbon monarchy
	had been restored,
but the king had fallen out with the army,
and was so unpopular that discord
broke out even among his supporters.
Napoleon knew about this, and saw
an opportunity for his return;
secretly, he embarked on the waters
of the Ligurian, reaching the shore
near Cannes. He was able at once to earn

the loyalty of those soldiers who served
	with him before,
and with an army he marched down the curved
boulevards of Paris not much more
than a fortnight after his escape
from Elba. All of Europe had declared
war on him by this time; he defeated
Blucher and the Prussians before the shape
of his future emerged. Field Marshalls glared
at battalions, worn and depleted,

in the field at Waterloo. A battle
    which might inspire
Napoleon's followers, and settle
the restoration of his old empire,
was about to take place. The British Duke
of Wellington, allied with the Prussian,
held the higher ground, and for once the skill
of the self-crowned emperor failed; he took
a heavy defeat, and soon was rushing
back to Paris, disorganised and ill.

At last he surrendered to the British
    at Rochefort
in Belgium. His captors remained skittish,
anxious that he might escape once more,
so after his second abdication
Napoleon was exiled to a place
as far over the globe as could be found.
He was left in lonely contemplation
of all that he had achieved in his days
as absolute ruler, and of the ground

he had set down for permanent reforms
    of the French law.
Sheltered from the fierce South Atlantic storms
by a row of pine trees, under the raw
island skies of St Helena, he led
a quiet life under guard. It lasted

just six years, however. Liver disease
or cancer meant Napoleon was dead
when not yet old, leaving only the wind-blasted
island and its stands of swaying trees.

Evolution

Charles Darwin was the grandson of a prince
among scientists, Erasmus Darwin,
    and the grandson, also,
of a king among crockery-makers,
one of the founders of the Industrial
Revolution, Josiah Wedgwood. Though
    he studied medicine
in Edinburgh, and divinity since
moving to Cambridge with its wide acres
of level farmland, where the natural

world would make a claim on his attention, he
was not a notable scholar. While there
    he came into contact
with a group of Cambridge scientists led
by John Stevens Henslow, the botanist
and cleric, and this meeting had an impact
    as he began to share
their interests. When an opportunity
arose to join the *Beagle*, Henslow said
that Darwin should be the naturalist

on its voyage to the South Pacific.
Planned to take two years, the journey lasted
    for five, and extended
as far as Australia, though at first

it was only meant to map and explore the coast
of South America. Darwin ended
    up among the plastered
sandstone of the half-built Sydney Town, traffic
bustling in the lanes and parks as if cursed,
the Harbour glittering under the most

clear sky imaginable. He went for a ride
into the Blue Mountains, and collected
    specimens wherever
he ventured forth. When he returned, at last,
to England, Darwin led an uneventful life,
becoming prone to weakness and fever.
    Soon he had selected
his cousin Emma Wedgwood as his bride,
after compiling a long, detailed list
of the benefits and drawbacks in a wife.

He moved from London to the countryside
of Kent, to cultivate his garden
    and conservatories;
he raised fowls and pigeons, as well as ten
children. For years he would make no attempt
to publish the developing theories
    which began to harden
in his mind as he considered the wide
implications of those things he often
observed from the *Beagle*; only to pre-empt

another scientist, Alfred Wallace,
did he bring *The Origin of Species*
        by Means of Natural
Selection before the public. It sold
out at once. Organic evolution
was an idea put forward by several
        thinkers, yet no precise
hypothesis had fitted into place
to explain how it might occur; for old
Erasmus Darwin, a poetic emotion

accompanied the idea. Rooted
in his observations both of fossil
        remains and of living
animals, Charles Darwin's theory proposed
that competition within a species
leads to the survival of those having,
        as an individual,
the advantageous traits most suited
to their circumstances. From the long-nosed
anteaters he had watched among the trees

of forest-shrouded South America
to the finches on Pacific islands
        with their colourful beaks,
he deduced the signs of adaptation.

The theory was accepted inside
most of the leading scientific cliques
     almost at once. The hands
which had gathered plants and exotica
from the earth's corners completed the elucidation
of his theory in three more books before he died.

Revolution

                    One of nine children
born in the Prussian
        city of Trier Karl Marx
                was the son of a bourgeois lawyer
and studied law himself: soon he found history
                and the philosophy
                    of Hegel much more to his taste
and because his studies were lagging behind
    the standards required in Berlin submitted
his dissertation
                        to the university in Jena
known for its laxness, then began
            contributing some articles
        to the *Rheinische Zeitung*
                    which he soon came to edit

Circulation trebled under his editorship
before Prussia's authorities
    suspended the newspaper
for being too outspoken in its virulent
attacks on the government Marx was already
a revolutionary

                nothing matters but the quality
of the affection –
in the end – that year he married Jenny
Von Westphalen

Believing theft to be the main principle in
        Government he moved to Paris and began to
associate with communist societies
where he met Friedrich Engels, who would be lifelong
             his collaborator and friend
      after two years he was expelled from Paris, moving
to Brussels and with Engels reorganised
                the London-based Communist League
        helping them to formulate a programme

    It took two months for Marx to write,
with Engels, *The Communist Manifesto*
          39 pages of propaganda
and intellectual brow-beating
        a masterpiece of
        its kind *The workers have nothing
to lose but their chains. They have a world to win*
          he was expelled from Brussels and went
        to London with the children

and his loyal wife

                ...nor would he move again

        nor could he bring himself to seek

        paid employment though he lived in poverty material
and spiritual

        for the following 14 years and three of his
children died

        a sacrifice to bourgeois misery while he sat in
the reading room

       *   *   *

    Beneath the domed ceilings of the British
Museum among the hidden stacks of government
        documents the books in glass-faced cases and leather
            bindings he acquired vast knowledge of economics
amid the wreckage of Europe

            Engels, on a mere clerk's wage, did his best
to support Marx and his starving progeny

*   *   *

When Engels was made a partner
        in his family's business his support
        became more generous and by this time
Marx had almost completed Volume I
of *Das Kapital*

        the only part
     of his three-volume *magnum opus*
        to be published in his lifetime An international
        figure after the Paris Commune Marx declined
in energy in the final decade
        of his life, spending much of his time at
                health resorts
before a lung abscess
        carried him off to be buried
        at Highgate on a hillside looking
     over London and its yellow haze, his monument
a statue on a white marble plinth

Inoculation

The year after the death of Napoleon
  Louis Pasteur was born in Dole,
Eastern France, a small commodious town
  with poplar trees along the whole

length of its winding river. The Pasteur
  family home had a prospect
of the valley, where market gardens were
  planted out to make precise, checked

forms. Louis went to school in Becancon,
  and then achieved his doctorate
in Paris, studying fermentation
  while he worked to consolidate

an academic career through teaching posts
  held at the university
of Strasbourg, and then Lille. At Strasbourg, his hosts
  introduced him to a Marie

Laurent, who was to become his wife.
  Next he became the professor
of chemistry in Paris, where his life
  soon revolved around research, for

the Emperor Napoleon III
  ordered a laboratory
at the Ecole Normale for him: official word
  indicated that his industry

deserved imperial support. There he showed
  fermentations are mainly due
to organisms in the air, and this bestowed
  new rules upon those vintners who

wanted to prevent wine disease, or to make
  their vinegar. Spontaneous
generation of disease could not take
  place, he proved, and laid the basis

for all modern bacteriology
  through these findings. Part-paralysed
before he was to reach the age of fifty,
  he kept working, and analysed

silkworm disease, injurious growths in beer,
  anthrax, and chicken cholera:
he showed there is less virulence to fear
  from these organisms in air,

or when they have been transmitted through various
  animals, or cultured in a
different way. He showed, through a famous
  experiment, that a thinner

attenuated bacillus of anthrax
  injected into sheep and cows
protected them from the disease. The facts
  proved in similar public shows

of "vaccination", as Jenner named the process,
  brought him national attention.
His most celebrated success
  came with the inoculation

of a nine-year-old boy who had been bitten
  by a rabid dog; the boy's life
was saved. The treatment, never forgotten
  when fatal distempers were rife

throughout the world, may have been the greatest
  single step which modern science
would take toward preserving lives; the latest
  developments, now, ever since

Pasteur's breakthrough, can be imagined
　　as the direct descendants
of that boy with the foaming dog, lined
　　up through the years like the pendants

awarded to victors at a country shoot.
　　Although in failing health, Pasteur
continued to work at his Institute
　　until death came without a cure.

Electromagnetism

Stomach cancer carried away the mother
of James Clerk Maxwell in her forties,
while her only child's tutor thought

he was slow at learning. Nonetheless,
the boy published his first scientific paper
when only fourteen years of age, and entered

the University of Edinburgh
two years later. Edinburgh, that town
of ancient stone, with its crags and grassy

spaces, always more pleasing to the eye
seen through a curtain of rain, was his home,
as it had been to many of the world's

most remarkable thinkers. At nineteen,
though, he moved to Cambridge, where his powers
began to obtain recognition:

his mathematics teacher said of Clerk
Maxwell that it seemed impossible
for him to think wrongly on any

physical subject. Not yet aged thirty,
he was awarded a professorship
in natural philosophy at King's

College, London, and began the most
fruitful years of his life. His two classic
papers on the electromagnetic

field were published, and his demonstration
of colour photography took place
at the same time as the Civil War

between the American States raged
in its progress. He retired to Scotland
when just in his early thirties, to work

on his treatise on electricity
and magnetism, though he continued
to visit London every spring.

He made major contributions to many
areas of physics: his essay
on the rings of Saturn, written when

he was in his twenties, gained confirmation
a century later from the Voyager
space-probe. Without his discoveries

much of the twentieth century
could not have taken place: his theory
of electromagnetic waves led to

the radio industry and all its
applications, from communication
and entertainment to medicine

and the military. With no electric power,
the cities of the world might be in darkness,
messages still delivered on horseback,

the gas-lit theatres crowded, novels
in the hands of patients in hospital
waiting rooms where diagnosis still relied

on guesswork. Clerk Maxwell contributed
to the founding of information
theory, and to cybernetics,

and to the theory of fluids; his work
in geometrical optics would later
enable the invention of the fish-eye lens.

He was only forty when elected
to the Cavendish professorship
at Cambridge, where Newton and Darwin

had lived before him, but after eight short
years, just like his mother, he was carried
to oblivion by a fatal stomach cancer.

ACKNOWLEDGEMENTS

Poems in this collection have appeared previously in print in
the following publications: *Best Australian Poems*, *Contrappasso*, and
Quadrant. The author is grateful for advice, encouragement and
inspiration from certain individuals, including Robert Gray, Harry
Cummins, Stephen McInerney, Geoffrey Lehmann, Jennifer and
Paul O'Brien, Alexa Moses, Stephen Carroll, Ursula Dubosarsky,
Theodore Ell, Margaret Connolly, Frances Grant and Emily Grant
(Jock Grant supplied the subject for "Immortal", but offered neither
advice nor encouragement).

The collection as a whole is dedicated to the memory of departed
friends; Christopher Koch, Kate Jennings, Les Murray, Alex Buzo,
Amy Witting and Mick Fuller.